Green Diesel Methadone

Hidden Addiction

May Cassidy

authorHOUSE®

AuthorHouse™ UK Ltd.
500 Avebury Boulevard
Central Milton Keynes, MK9 2BE
www.authorhouse.co.uk
Phone: 08001974150

First published by AuthorHouse   3/29/2010

ISBN: 978-1-4389-9333-1 (sc)

This book is printed on acid-free paper.

Contents

References

AGR AN O FF, B.W. (1967) memory and protein synthesis .Scientific American 216,115 -112

AK ERS, R.L. (1992) drugs alcohol and society. Belmont, CA: Wordsworth

Av ER III J. R. 1982 anger and aggression: New York: Springer

Baker, T. B. Morse, E., and Sherman, J. E. 1986 the motivation to use drugs: A psychological Analysis of urges

Barker, G. H. 1987 psychological factors and immunity. Journal of psychosomatic research 31,1-10

Benson, H. And Stuart, E.M. 1993 the wellness book. New York: Simon and Schuster

Birch, H. G. Rabinowitz in, H. S. 1951 the negative effect of previous experience on productive thinking. Journal of experimental psychology, 41,121 -124

Blame, S. B. 1991 the problem of quantifying alcohol consumption. British Journal of addiction, 86, 1059 -1060

Bonate, P. L. 1991. Serotonin receptors subtypes: functional Physiological, and clinical correlates clinical neuropharmacology, 14,116.

Bower, G. H. 1981 mood and memory- American psychologist, 36 129 -148.

Cannon, W. B. 1929 body changes in pain, hunger, fear and rage second edition. New York: Appleton - century -- Crofts.

Davis, J. M. 1974 A two factor theory of schizophrenia. Journal of psychiatric research, 11,25- 29

Davis, K. L, Kahn, R. S. Ko. G., and Davidson, M. 1991 dopamine in schizophrenia: American Journal of psychiatry, 148,1474 -1486

Delmonte, M. M. 1990 medication and change: mindfulness versus regression. Australian Journal of clinical hydrotherapy 57 – 64

Dodge , K. A. 1993 social - cognitive mechanisms in the development of conduct disorder and depression. Annual review of psychology 44,559 - 584

Elkins, R. L. 1991 An appraisal of chemical aversion approaches to alcoholism treatment. Behaviour research and therapy 29,387 - 413

Goteborgs, U. 1990 schizophrenia: A sub- cortical neurotransmitter imbalance syndrome: schizophrenia bulletin, 16,425 - 432.

American psychiatric Association 1987. Diagnostic and statistical manual of mental disorders Washington DC. Th e fourth addition.

Abramson, L Y. Garber, J. Edwards. N. and Seligman, M. E. P. 1978 expectancy change in depression and schizophrenia Journal of abnormal psychology 87,165 -179

Albert's, B. Bray, D LEWIS, RA FF. M. Roberts, K. and Watson, JD. 1989 molecular biology of the cell. New York Garland.

Abramson, L.Y. Metalsky, G. I. And Alloy, L. B. 1989 hopelessness depression: psychological review, 96, 358 - 372

Alexander,, C. N. Rainforth, M. V. & Gelderloos ,P. 1991 transcendental meditation, self-actualization, and psychological health: a conceptual overview and statistical meta- analysis. Journal of social behaviour and personality. But the 189 - 247.

Averill, J. R. 1982 anger aggression: an essay of emotion. New York: Springer - Verfag.

American psychiatric Association 1994 diagnostic and statistical manual of mental disorders third edition Washington, DC: APA.

Altman, Lawrence K. 1990 the evidence mounts on passive smoking, New York Times (may) 29: B5

Anglin, M. Douglas 1988 the efficiency of civil commitment in treating narcotic addiction pages 8 --34 in compulsory treatment of drug abuse: research and clinical practice Rockville, M.D: national Institute on drug abuse

Treatment of drug abuse, pages 393 - 460 in drugs and crime, Michael Tonry and James Q. Person Wilson. Chicago: University of Chicago press

Louis S. Harris. Rockville. M.D.: National Institutes of Health abuse: the impact of Herod addiction upon criminality pages 160 — 69.

Blackmore, John. 1979 diagnosis heroin addiction. Prescription methadone xorrection magazine December: 24-.31.

New York Times August 15: B. 10 popular drugs may damage the brain.

Bloom, Floyd E. brain we search for today and tomorrow: recent advances and research frontiers. Page 9 - 26. International Research conference on biochemical approaches to elicit drug demand reduction, US Government printing office. DC:

Blum, Richard H. And Associates 1969 society and drugs. San Francisco: Jossey - Bass substance abuse prevention: theory, practice and effectiveness, pages 461 - 519 in drugs and crime Michael Tonry and James Q. Wilson Chicago University of Chicago press;

Louis H. Blair 1990 substances use and delinquency among inner-city adolescent males, Washington DC: urban Institute.

Comorbidity of substance abuse and other site psychiatric disorders in adolescence and: American Journal of psychiatry. September: 1131 - 41 Burkstine, Oscar. David A. Kaminer ,Y.

Burns, John F. 1995 heroin becomes source for 1.5 million in Pakistan and your times April 5:4.

Afghans: now they Blame America: New York Times Magazine, February 4.23 — 29,37.

Bowden, Mark. 1987 Dr. Dealer, New York: Warner books.

Chambers, Carl D. and Leon Brill. 1973 methadone: experiences and issues. New York: behavioural publications

Childress, Ann Rose. 1993 medication in drug abuse treatment, summary in NIDA sconce national conference on drug abuse research and practice: an alliance for the 21st-century pages 73-75

Rockville, MD. national Institute on drug abuse.

Childress, Ann Rose. A. Thomas Mclellan, Charles P. O'Brien 1985 behavioural therapies for substance abuse: international Journal of the addictions 20:947 - 69

Delong, James V. treatment and rehabilitation 1972 pages 173 - 254 in dealing with drug abuse: a report to the Ford foundation: New York: Prager.

Dole, Vincent P. And Marie Nyswander. 1966 rehabilitation of heroin addicts after blockage with methadone. New York State Journal of medicine April: 2011 - 17.1965 1965 a medical treatment for Diacetyl morphine heroin addiction. Journal of the American medical Association 193(August) 146 - 50

Harris,Louis S., 1994 problems of drug dependency, 19 93, volume 1. Rockville, MD. nationa Institute on drug abuse.

Institute for the study of drug dependency (isdd) 1987 drug abuse briefing, London:

Judson, Barbara A. And Avarm Goldstein. 1986 uses of Naloxone in the diagnosis and treatment of heroin addiction. Pages 1 =18 in research on the treatment of narcotic addiction: state of-the-art edited by James R. Cooper. Fred Altman, Barry S. BROWN, and Dorynne

Czechowicz. Rockville, *MD;* national Institute on drug abuse. 1988 more Afghan opium: Less in Pakistan. New York Times April 14:6

Kaplan, John 1983 drugs and crime: legal aspects pages 643 — 52 in the Encyclopaedia of crime and justice. Edited by San ford H. Kadish. New York: Free Press. 1974 heroin use as an attempt to cope: clinical observations. American Journal of psychiatry 131 February: 160 - 64.

Elizabeth Kolbert, communities halt narcotics clinic. New York Times: September 30:89.

Bibring, E. 1953, the mechanics of depression .In P.Greenacre affective disorders page 13 - 48 New York: international University press.

BROWN, G. W. And Harris 1978 social origins of depression: a study of psychiatric disorders in women. London: Tavistock.

Chauduri, H. 1965 philosophy and meditation New York: philosophical Library. Okay and I References

Akers R. L. (1992)drugs alcohol and society Belmont ,ca. Wordsworth.

Agranoff, B. W. (1967) memory and protein synthesis Scientific c American, 216, 115-122 American Psychiatric Association (1990)

Baker, T, B. Morse E, & Sherman, J. E. (1986) the motivation to use drugs: A psychological analysis of urges. 34, 257-323

Benson, H. 7 Stuart, E.M. (1993) the wellness book. New York; Simon & Schuster

Barker, G. H. (1987) psychological Factors and immunity; Journal of Psychosomatic research 31, 1-10

Blume, S. B. (1991) the problems of quantifying alcohol consumption British Journal of addiction. 86, 1059—1060

Bonate, P. L (1991) Serotonin receptors : clinical Neuropharmacology 14, 1-16

Bower, G. H. Mood and memory. American Psychologist, 36, 129-148

Janice Keller Phelps M.D., Alan E. Nourse, M D.

The e Hidden Addiction and how to get free

Suzanne Diamond "Alleviating Addictions : Herbs That Help", Healthy and Natural Journal 6; 5 issues 3o (october31,1999): 101-03

Michael Lesser, M. D. Nutrition and vitamin therapy New York; Bantam, 1981, 109-111

Melvyn R. Werbach, M.D. Nutritional influences on illness;

A sourcebook of clinical research . Tarzana, CA, third line press 1994.

Healing mood disorders with essential fatty acids, doctors prescription for healthy living. Natural healing for schizophrenia and other common mental disorders, Eugene Or, Borage books 2001: 86

James F. Balch, M. D., and Phyllis A, Balch C.N.C. prescription for nutritional healing, Garden City Park . N.Y. Avery Publishing Group (1990)

Sherry A. Rogers, depression, 94.

Elkins Rita, depression and natural medicine: a nutritional approach to depression and mood swings; Pleasant Groves, UT. Woodland Publishing (1995)

Eve Edelman, Natural healing for schizophrenia and other common mental disorders, Neurotransmitters and amino Acids

World Health Organization, acupuncture review and analysis of reports on controlled clinical trials (2003) page(-9-10)

The 1991 census page (HmSO) 1993 limiting long-term illness for Great Britain.

Birch, S. J. Felt R.L. understanding acupuncture, Edinburgh, Churchill Livingstone 1999

Bridges, L. face reading and Chinese medicine, Edinburgh Churchill Livingstone 2004.

Franyzis, B.K. opening the energy gates of your body Barkley, California: North Atlantic books 1993.

Hicks, A. 5 secrets of health unhappiness, London: Thomson's 2001.

Lewith, G. T. a puncture, its place in Western medical science, Edinburgh: Churchill, Livingstone 1999.

Lu, H, the yellow Emperor's book of acupuncture: Vancouver, Academy of Oriental heritage, 1973.

Stone, I., the healing factor: vitamins C. against disease, New York: Gromet & Dunlop in 1972.

Fabris, N. AIDS. Seeing deficiency and Thematic hormone failure: Journal of the American Medical Association volume 259, 839 -- 40 1998.

Hansen, M. A. Fernandes, G. and Good, R. A. nutrition and immunity: the influence of diet on autoimmune and the role of zinc in the immune response: annual review of nutrition volume. 2,151 - 771982, Denied

Foreword

This book is written and dedicated to the methadone taker; It is an informative guide for methadone users, their families, and society at large. It is not a self help book as coming off methadone should never be undertaken without medical supervision. There is nothing strange or eccentric in this work only a new perspective to an unhealthy and unnatural method of treating opium addiction with another drug, one perhaps more addictive

Its purpose is to empower those taking methadone to examine the long term effects of methadone on their overall health, that by focusing on nutrition, vitamins and minerals they can increase their chances to come off this potent drug.

The knowledge gathered here has been around for a long time but for some reason it has been ignored, perhaps due to the fact that methadone is the only source we have that appears to accommodate society's moral code, while giving the user the illusion of ensuring a healthy mental and psychical existence.

My thanks to the participants of R.A.S.P. Whom I have the pleasure to work with. I cannot commend them enough on their courage, trust, intellect, and creativity especially Paul Mc Donald for his inspiration in naming this book.

Coming off methadone is dramatic, this book attempts to encourage those on methadone that they may improve their physical and mental health in preparation with their doctor. By eating foods rich in the Vitamins, Minerals, Essential fatty fats and Amino Acids that can help with withdrawal symptoms. The correct diet, reduction of stressors, by means of holistic measures exercise, learning life skills allows the individual to regain control over their lives

There- fore increasing the chance of better life changes leading to an independence and positive thought processes. Continuous use of controlled methadone does not empower the methadone individual, on the contrary it sends a strong message that the person is helpless, dependent, sick, different, unable to function without his or her green diesel.

As a society we need to indulge ourselves passionately in the undertaking, understanding and care of the dangers of illegal drug use and the growing menace of treating minor ailments such as stress with prescribed medication. Until we do we shall have a growing antisocial, unnatural, obsessive and unhealthy attitude, not to mention a legal drugs epidemic in society.

A new outlook to an old and unworkable problem is needed. It is my intention in this book to enlighten those on methadone about the importance of nutrients, vitamins, minerals, which are important in the manufacturing of amino acids and essential fat for brain fuel. The large pharmaceutical companies who deal mainly in synthetic chemicals making large profits on the backs of misery as strung out individuals seek the road to normality and respect though Methadone use.

We have lost the wisdom of our ancestors who knew the importance of the humble cabbage, that vegetables, fruit, protein all contributed to mental health, That a man's wealth was measured not in money or the crack ,but in a fertile brain, that intellectual abilities survives better on food grown without Pesticides, Fungicides, processed foods or potatoes steeped in oil. These facts significantly are tragically lost to the growing number of Methadone users and doctors who treat them.

Green Diesel

Green Diesel or Molly is the street name given to Methadone which is used throughout Ireland to treat individuals who have an addiction to heroin. This magic bullet as is was know, was discovered during the Second World War. Hitler upon finding his country's access to morphine in short supply that other well know opioid, a full cousin to both heroin and codeine, set his scientists the task of developing a drug that would produce the same effects as morphine. Later to become methadone. Hitler was a man who liked to be obeyed, his demand was met and so Dolophine was born and the rest is history.

But what do we know about the medical side effects of this powerful narcotic drug that over ten thousand young people in Ireland alone is given on a daily basis, of between 80mg to 120 mg depending on the severity of their heroin habit

The national drugs strategy set out in 2001-2008 informs us that it was developed with the co-. operation and input with certain state bodies as well as voluntary and community groups. These are placed in the drug affected areas throughout the country. Mostly in the most deprived areas in Ireland. England, and Scotland,

The health service is responsible for the rehabilitation, addiction counselling, detoxification programmes, and methadone treatment centres. This body introduced Green Diesel as an alternative to Heroin which was devastating the younger generation who appeared to have strolled down the unending path of drugging. This powerful narcotic works by stopping the withdrawal symptoms and cravings associated with heroin abuse, it allows the person addicted to heroin to obtain his narcotic legally therefore is acceptable to society.

Minister knows best so when in 1997 the then minster of Health and children Brain Cowan (now Irelands Taoiseach) announced that the good practice in the prescribing, dispensing, and control of methadone were to be put in place. No one batted an eyelid or questioned the effects of this new drug. The concept that we would rid our streets of an avalanche of drugs appealed to the masses.

His statement reads

"I welcome the fact that GPs and Pharmacists are involved in prescribing methadone in the treatment of opiate abuse.

The review body included representation from the pharmaceutical society, and general practitioners, plus members from the health board An interesting lobby in their quest for a cure to the ravishing abuse that is ripping the heart out of the most vulnerable and deprived areas in Irish society.

One could be inclined to beg the question "who benefits" Surly not those who must drink a daily dose of between eighty and one hundred and twenty mils of this green sugar laced glue to ensure that they can function in their daily lives

Ignorance concerning methadone abounds not only by the individual who consumes this opioid, but by most physicians, nurses, and many medical professionals who are unaware that this addictive substance is as potent as heroin. Methadone is a psychoactive drug meaning it produces an effect on both mind and brain. Drugs are taken either orally, intravenously, or rectal (inserted by the back passage) some drugs are passed quickly from the body by the kidneys; others can build up in fatty tissues in the body. Drugs come in many forms, tablets, capsules, lozenges, liquids, (methadone comes under this category)

The official FDA information regarding this drug refers to it as Methadone Hydrochloride, and reports that each tablet contains dibasic calcium, Phosphate, Microcrystalline cellulose, magnesium sterate, colloidal silicon, Pregelatinized starch, and Stearic acid.

What are these ingredients and what do they mean for the methadone user.

Magnesium Stearate is made by hydrogenating cotton seed or palm oil, its purpose is the use in the supplement industry as lubricants. By adding it to raw material it ensures that machinery runs at maximum speed. As fatty substances it is used as diluents in the manufacture of medical tablets, capsules, and powers. Its lubricating properties ensure that the ingredients do not stick to equipment during the process of compressing chemicals into tablets. It is also used in sweets, and baby formulas in pure power form. The substance is reported to be dangerous, and the dust can be an explosion hazard (nice to know).

It is A bovine filler in the manufacture of capsules and tablets such as vitamins.

It goes through a process of hydrogenation, meaning the oil is extracted by subjection to strong heat at high temperatures in the presents of a metal catalyst for several hours, this creates a saturated fat(referred to in later captures) Hydrogenated vegetable fats contain altered molecules derives from fatty acids and may be toxic.

Decreased absorption can be a problem also. The Pharmaceutical Technology Journal reported that the use of this substance reduced the absorption of nutrients from 90% to 25% with the use of Stearates. The most startling fact to emerge concerning the use of this lubricant is the effect it can have on the T-cells which is a component of the immune system. This is stated clearly in the Journal Immunology (1990) T- cells are released by the immune system whenever it fails to recognize a foreign substance entering the body,(we see this with allergic reactions to certain foods such as gluten a protein found in wheat, nuts, milk,) and a host of other foods we shall deal with later. In order for Magnesium Stearate to be used in manufacturing, companies need to gain a safety compliance order from the Environmental Protection Agency as it comes under the classification of a hazardous substance.

This substance is also used in paint, varnish drier, binder emulsifier (used in some cosmetics).If inhaled it can irritate the respiratory tract while ingestion may cause gastroenteritis.

Methadone Hydrochloride (hydrochlorides)are salts resulting from the acid with an organic base (amines) these come from protein breakdown or fermentation of certain foods and fruits, ,large amounts can be found in cheese, chocolate, wines, beer, yeast extracts, fish products, fruits, vegetables such as bananas, avocados, tomatoes, and butter beans.

An amine : a nitrogen atom that connects to 3 hydrogen's it may also be connected to a benzene ring, a phenol, a salicylate or many other things in the body.

Ammonia is the core structure of Amine and many of our neurotransmitters are amines. Amino acids and histamine released during an allergic reaction is an amine.

It is interesting to note that during times of stress or hormonal change we can become more sensitive to some of the foods we ingest.

It is also interesting that Amine is part and parcel of a substance used in the manufacturing process of methadone, and the number of individuals partaking of this green diesel has allergies ranging from wheat, milk, asthma being the most common. We also receive Amines in skin, hair products, and these are reported to be toxic when inhaled or absorbed. In future captures I shall give a list of foods and products containing both Amines and Sallicylate and which are also know to cause food intolerance.

No 2) Starch is a product that is reminiscent with the eighteenth century when our great-grand parents sprayed starch on cloths to stiffen them. Starch is also part of methadone it is a major carbohydrate reserve in plant tubers and seed endosperm and is found in food especially potatoes Sugar beet, grains corn and wheat. It is made up of glucose. This process is carried out by special proteins called (enzymes) in the body for their conversion into energy. Whenever we eat complex carbohydrates insulin releases sugar slowly into the body ensuring we are not getting a sugar rush followed by a drop that can affect mood, or appetite.

.blood sugar swings are the result of fast releasing sugars found in most refined carbohydrates or processed foods. High sugar intake has a knock on effect of releasing hormones such as insulin, adrenaline and cortisol, when sugar levels drop we get the heave hoving of blood sugar levels leaving us with cravings for more refined carbs, could be the result of that large rubber tyre around the Methadone users middle.

Starch is converted into sugar by enzymes in the body, it is a component of Methadone it is also added to the number of manufactured foods in the super market these are dressed up in the disguise of (Fructose, Glucose, Dextrose, Lactose found in milk)

If the methadone individual consumes between 80 to 100 mls of green diesel per day it adds up to a hell of a lot of sugar and all that before a cup of tea or cornflakes is eaten. I have known some of those on methadone to find stress un-manageable and we know that blood sugar highs and lows is responsible for releasing stress hormones into the blood stream to counteract this effect which in turn results in a build up of fat around the wrist.

No3 cellulose is a lot stronger than starch it is one of the many polymers found in nature. Wood paper and cotton all contain cellulose. It is made of repeat units of the monomer glucose. Which as we saw above the body metabolizes in order for us to survive? Cellulose is built from sugar.

Scientists inform us that glucose units in starch are connected to alpha linkages where as the glucose units in cellulose are connect by beta linkages. This makes a lot of difference, you cannot eat cellulose but you can eat starch. We saw how starch is broken down in the body by enzymes, but the human body is devoid of enzymes that break down cellulose unless you happen to be a cow with four bellies or a termite who can chew through wood.

Cellulose is used to make fibres for rope and clothing and it does not dissolve in water, therefore making it difficult to absorb.

For drugs to enter the central nervous system they must pass or penetrate the blood brain barrier. Opioids have a configuration called the pipe riding ring making them compatible with the receiving neuron(specialized cell) endorphin. These endogenous peptides are protein fragments consisting of amino acids. These occur in the body as hormones, and endorphins produced naturally to relieve pain. They do so by activating natural opioid receptors in the nervous system. These have a similar chemical structure to morphine and are released to regulate contractions, determine mood while releasing certain hormones.

When drugs are administered it reaches certain barriers before reaching specific cells, this cell wall regulate oxygen and nutrients in the cell while waste products such as carbon dioxide and hormones out of the cell.

Drugs must be soluble in fat to pass through the cell membrane which are fat molecules coated by a protein layer.

As soon as a drug enters the blood stream by way of the small intestine it is then carried to the liver where it may be broken down for use in the body. It enters the circulation and is carried around the body. Methadone is a synthetic opioid mimicking the body's endorphins.

Insufficient protein can result in inadequate levels of peptides hormones.

Amino acids are needed to make neurotransmitters. A lack of protein is reported to result in diabetes, obesity, bone loss, fatigue, sexual dysfunction, these are symptoms I encounter in methadone users every day.

Hair and, nails, are made from long protein chains know as Keratins. Horses, cows, birds, all need protein for the manufacture of hoofs, bone or enamel.

The pituitary gland is referred to as the lord of the glands, it regulates the release of hormones for metabolism. Hormone functioning is dependent on ACTH a natural chemical, that in turn sets off a string of actions for release of hydrocortisone which controls the body's fats, proteins, and carbohydrates allowing the body to cope with stress. Disturbance of the adrenal gland can cause an increase or decrease of hormones resulting in Addison's disease, know as an autoimmune disorder.

Because methadone is stored in the liver and released slowly into the blood stream it is deemed the god of opioids ,the liver then is the secret of methadone's long life, and the higher the dose the more the liver must store. The liver is the storehouse of this potent opioid. Perhaps this is one of the reasons some individual methadone users believe they can abstain from this green diesel for short periods only to find this can lead to re-use of heroin or relapse. This is extremely dangerous and can lead to over dose.

Another concern is that a damaged liver such as hepatitis, or H.I.V., because the metabolism process does not work properly. Therefore methadone is excreted by the body and can lead to withdrawal symptoms, or the person receiving larger doses of this opioid, and according to the methadone official FDA. Methadone is extensively evaluated in patients with hepatic insufficiency, those with liver impairment may be at risk of accumulating methadone after multiple dosing.

Warnings from this body reports that respiration depression is the chief hazard associated with methadone hydrochloride administration, this is due to the depressant effects occurring later and persisting longer than its peak analgesic effect.

Extreme caution to those with conditions accompanied by hypoxia, (an inadequate supply of oxygen to the tissues, this can result from strenuous exercise) asthma, chronic pulmonary disease, sleep apnoea syndrome (the person has of cessation of breathing) severe obesity, Laboratory tests show that methadone inhibits cardiac potassium channels, prolonging the QT effect associated with higher doses of methadone

Certain prescribed drugs can interact with methadone, those on lithium which can be toxic in itself must be careful.

Cognitive tasks, of taking the children to school, shopping for food, paying bills, running for a bus is not an easy task with a belly full of Molly, especially as it has similar side effects as heroin, sweats, nausea, drowsiness, vomiting and the lack of having a good shit due to constipation. All that, considering we are leaving out the build up of toxicity in the liver, rotten teeth due to the content of sugar, diabetes can also be attributed to high sugar intake as the medical profession is now warning the general populous. Osteoporosis that disease which is associated with older women who have gone over the hill in the child bearing sense, is now prevalent in a number of those prescribed this legal drug.

The hidden dangers associated with methadone was evident with the publicity surrounding the death of Daniel Smith the 20 year old son of model Anna Nicola Smith as a result of Methadone. In Ireland the Dublin City Coroner released statistics which showed that 14 people died from Methadone with another 19 deaths associated to the drug, in comparison to heroin related deaths, which was 14 actual deaths and 14 associated with heroin.

Methadone's therapeutically attributes do not appear to stack up when we look at the growing concerns associated with this potent drug.

In order to treat someone with chronic alcoholism, who was suffering with serious liver damage, the prognosis would be to abstain from alcohol.

How is it safe to treat an addiction with a stronger addictive substance as a means of detoxification?"

I'm a monkey's uncle if it works."

Would it be more accurate to suggest that the real reason for keeping thousands of individuals on this addictive substance be the beneficial results of keeping crime rates down, which has the added benefit for society, less taxes having to be dished out in the name of keeping certain strands of society strung out of their brains on a legal drug, that is now known to cause drug related death, in those taking it for physical and emotional pain.

This wonder drug is only wonderful in that those in desperate need of an opioid don't have to snatch old ladies handbags to feed their dependency on a manmade substance, one that is reaping massive profits for manufacture, dispenser, and prescriber.

The facts speaks for themselves in that large bucks are to be had for the continuous dispensing of Methadone, add to this the method of fermentation carbohydrates (sugars) with substances that are known to not only raise sugar levels in the body, but to release an invasion of insulin to counteract high sugar intake. Following hot on its heels is the release of adrenaline and cortisol.

Food allergies due to the increase of salicyate and Amine, and Glutamate, all due to protein breakdown in the fermentation process

The once indigent doctor, who ran the heroin abuser from his surgery, with as little respect as a Rhino, is now keen to welcome them unto their books as a patient.

The long term effects of methadone are not fully understood or explored by the scientific community, it is for this reason I feel compelled to write this book, both as a concern for the menace in out mist, and as a mark of respect to those methadone participants that 1 have the honour to work with in ensuring they take back control of their lives. I shall explore the hidden dangers, and side effects I have witnessed in my work as a psychotherapist, counselling those who deservedly want to detoxify from the perils of continuous use for eight to ten years.

Side effects are an everyday occurrence, but some in the medical profession prefer to ignore, or turn a blind eye, for reasons known only to themselves.

Liver toxicity, metabolism disturbance, brittle bones, rotten and missing teeth, and weight gain can be so bad that you feel you are giving the Michelin man a free ride around your belly, depression, constipation, bloating, and perhaps diabetes due to the high sugar content and disturbance in calcium balance. We can now apparently add death to a cure, that appears to be worse that the problem it was intended to solve.

Heroin
On the nod
─────────

Heroin is injected ,smoked, or inhaled it is an opiate that resembles a natural neurotransmitter called endorphins, these are the body's natural pain blockers, when a person abuses heroin over a long period of time these endorphins can become depleted,.

Because heroin works on the central and autonomic

Nervous system. It is a psychoactive drug meaning it changes or alters mood,and affects behaviour by working on specific biochemical ways in the brain. The brain being a major organ of the nervous system.

Heroin is highly addictive, producing tolerance after a short period of time resulting in a need for greater amounts for the user to acquire the same effect or high.

When heroin is discontinued the user suffers from withdrawals a combination of vomiting, sever stomach cramps, headache, shaking, as the body goes into freefall in its need to remain homeostatic.

According to science they are now able to recognize more than seventy neurotransmitters that are capable of binding in a duel way to receptor sites in the brain, which can act as inhibitors, or excitatory(cocaine is an excitatory)proactive drugs are devious, they fool the brain into believing it is receiving a natural chemical.

The breakthrough by pharmacology opened the flood gates for the culture of a pill for every ill.

We have over ten billion to a trillion brain cells in the brain, which work like clockwork orange in unison with the central nervous system.

The peripheral nervous system consists of the nerves that connect the brain and spinal cord to other parts of the body, which is divided into the somatic and autonomic system, that is in turn connected to and from our internal organs. It regulates heart, digestion, and breathing.

Heroin like morphine relieve pain, it changes consciousness ensuring that those who use it can drown out all anxiety, a good indicator that these individuals do not handle stress well nor have they acquired coping skill. Heroin changes mood one of the reasons it prompts people to abuse it.

Once hooked the ride becomes dangerous, its hazards are many, social life deteriorates, personal relationships fall apart as the heroin life style

7

consumes the individual taking this potent drug.

Death can result by way of overdose; the person suffocates due to depression of the brains respiratory centre.

Acquired immune deficient syndrome (AIDs) hepatitis is common in those using heroin.

Heroin presents its user with sensations of pleasure it is unusual to find someone abusing heroin to become aggressive as long as they can pay for their habit

Once consumed it is almost impossible to come off this opiate as its stranglehold tightens around your neck. This is also prevalent with methadone taking, the individual is faced with the dilemma of ambivalance,they want to stop, but don't want to stop. They fear the withdrawal symptoms associated with the drug. This resistance is compounded by the vulnerability of a life time of drugging.

They are denied a safe environment to express concerns such as having little or no education, they may have been abused, or lived in families where alcohol was a learned experience, manifesting itself whenever a crisis arose.

Heroin always reaches a crescendo

It becomes the crème ad la crème life revolves around it.

Criticism feeds it, defence mechanisms go into operation, and denial helps it take hold of the user allowing it to bind to the neurotransmitters as the body needs more and more.

Stopping the habit is lost somewhere between a hard place and a rock.

The dye is set in place for a life time of misery.

Brown Eyes

The body's tolerance which is described as its ability to adapt to the effects of a drug that is used at regular intervals, tolerance develops as the body becomes progressively immune to the chemical effects of the drug.

Our gaols which were once deemed as a safe place to lock away those who committed A crime or refused to conform to societies increasing regulations, can now become strung out on gear, snoozing away their time at the invitation of the government and Brain Cowan, who was the then minister of health and children when it was agreed to set-up the now famous Methadone treatment centres in an effort to save the next generation from self destruction. So what are heroin users putting into their bodies.

Heroin is an Eastern brown eyed immigrant the first to arrive on these shores before the tiger had the opportunity to roar. Its poppy seedpod is all that remains once it's beautiful soft red, pink or white flower falls on the harsh rugged domain of a distant land. The overlord grows the crop which is harvested by farmers. He counts out the Meany money to underpaid labourers, who slice incisions along the pregnant pods enabling the release of the milky white fluid to form and harden to a dark brown gum.

Labourers with deep corrugated lines etched into their leather foreheads as they wilt under the scorching sun collecting this raw gold. By using a flat knife they scrap it, gather it in bundles for the strenuous battering it must endure. Preparation or the process of purifying it is done with great precision in the overlords rush to extract the maximum money for his golden crop. It is then scrubbed like a child about to embark on a journey, to relatives that are seeing it for the first time.

This drug of choice is first dunked in lime or calcium oxide to give it its correct name, mixed with hot water in deep drums which dissolves the opium. Fertilizer is added moving it to the next process of mixing it with Ammonia .The chemist continues to mix pure Heroin with a certain amount of Morphine to the same measure of Acetic Acid which is then heated to one hundred and eighty degrees. The finished product is pure Heroin.

Water and Chloroform help to get rid of the impurities the last stage consists of the chemist adding Sodium Carbonate which leaves the particles to form. These are then placed in Alcohol, Ether, and Hydrochloric Acid.

This cocktail of death is almost ready for its journey of destroying the neurotransmitters of healthily young people, sent from Afghans with love in a hands across the sea approach...

Drug war lords give it a safe passage to its hiding places thought-out the world, while those selling it could be complimented on their selling techniques.

Heroin is an economical commodity, both for the dark skinned over-lord, and the designer clad young man or woman who believe they have developed the marketing skills of a Cobra. One missed payment and you get struck fully into the fangs danger or a servere beating. Addiction follows, as easy as the first puff .Once in the belly of this snake it is almost impossible to emerge without some type of damage. The once friendly hood becomes the terminator as his face expands like a puffer fish, in his anger and rage when you inform him you can't come up with the lolly. His once round pleading eyes disappear between robin red cheeks, eyes narrowed into slits as threats charge from his mouth in their attempt as keeping up with his sluggish thoughts. The journey has begun and the individual spirals down into a drug lifestyle trying to hold unto reality with their chipped finger nails. Once on the heroin boat the waves are rocky and life threading at best, death at worse, by way of dirty needles, H.i.v. homelessness, and mental illness.

The drug intended to block out the emotional pain, becomes a large rock around the individuals neck. The only way out is cold turkey or methadone that can take as little or as long as the individuals fear of withdrawal .

Old Man Liver

The liver secrets bile that helps it to break down fats. When the bile salt is lacking in certain nutrients the result is a build up of, chemicals, toxins, certain medications also have this affect on the brain. As we read in the previous captures the reason methadone has a life span of 24 hours is due to the livers ability to store it.

If the body is fed a constance stream of Methadone, Sleeping pills, Valium, Hash, Cocaine, Alcohol, Coffee, Cigarettes, and a host of over the counter drugs, it fails to do its job which results in the build-up of toxins.

The individual attending a Methadone clinic will be slugging anything between eighty and one Hundred and twenty mils a day. Plus they may consume alcohol and spirits several times a week. A good percentage shall have hepatitis, so the liver is on overload, as it fails to process the wide range of chemicals such as proteins for blood plasma or cholesterol and the proteins needed to carry fat around the body. Bile needed to remove waste or for absorption of fats in the small intestine ,the brain needs fatty acid for carrying neurotransmitter messagess.A malfunctioning liver cannot clear the blood of the many toxins and poisons we take into our body in the form of fumes,smoke,pesticides,fungicides which are sprayed on crops. Toxins are absorbed through the skin, nose, inhaled, or eaten in the form of food with bacteria.

The daily grind of pollutants, fast food, Pesticides, chemicals sprayed on vegetables, fruit imported from countries that don't have as stringent regulations regarding the use of chemicals as ourselves, chemicals in water, the list is endless and can only add to an already serious health hazard on the individual who is fed an opioid to wean them off an opioid because it is economical.

Prescribed drugs also add to the livers inability to cope, the drug Lipitor which is used to treat Cholesterol comes with the warning that it can cause liver damage, especially when taken with other drugs, birth control, hormone replacement therapy, and a host of others, all contribute to a congested sluggish liver.

The liver is responsible for over four hundred tasks, from filtering out waste, controlling hormonal balance it needs to remain in a healthy condition for the individuals well being. This brown reddish organ lies in the upper abdominal cavity. It has two lobes surrounded by the hepatic artery, which supplies the liver with oxygenated blood. The portal vein supports and supply's nutrient rich blood.

This organs importance in the body cannot be dismissed, as it processes and products a wide range of chemical substances which include life supporting proteins for blood. It also produces cholesterol and proteins that carry fat around the body,

Its task is to eliminate and break down toxins that we ingest, absorb or take in through our skin, or senses. A net work of ducts carries bile from the liver to the gallbladder, and the small intestine.

Bile plays an important role for the liver working with the gallbladder (they work as a team) removing waste and helping with the absorption of fats in the small intestine.

If bile is thickened or congested by a build up of chemicals it fails to do the job it was intended for, fat cannot be broken down leaving the person with a roll of fat like a second belly around the midriff.

This fatty liver syndrome is a sign that your liver is not working properly, the reason being that you are consuming too many carry -outs, Chinese, deep fat foods and processed shelf life food full of flavouring with Salicylate, Amine and Glutamate.

This wonder organ converts Amino Acids from the food we eat to protein these are important for Sending hormones into the blood stream. Whenever our hormones are out of balance we retain fluid, crave certain foods and get a bloated feeling.

Toxins are the dreaded curse to the liver, as we see with alcohol, prolonged and excessive use of this potent drug causes liver damage which if neglected can destroy it.

Prescribed drugs can be a silent threat to the liver, while we read the leaflet on the side effects we find ourselves in a no win situation because we need the medication to function.

I became interested in this topic due to having to take medication for an under active thyroid gland, high cholesterol, acid in the stomach, osteoporosis, this was interesting in that the inability of the gland to manufacture thyroxin was sending my cholesterol through the roof, but by taking the medication for the thyroid and cholesterol which were causing my bones to become brittle. On seeking answers to this dire situation from my specialist I was informed I had to continue taking them.

To add insult to injury I started to develop a lump of fat around my wrist. I resembled my dead father's belly whenever it was swollen with a cancerous growth, the size of a football stadium.

When we have an unhealthy liver it can result in a build up of toxins a serious lack of enzymes (the group of complex proteins needed for biochemical reactions within the body)this in turn can result in confusion,tiredness,mood swings or, depression. A visit to the doctor can result in anti-depressants, to get you over the hump, while your poor liver is screaming "I can't cope with the overload".

Coffee is another stimulant, this fluffy Italian national drools at you with a helping of delicious chocolate swimming on the top of the cup. Cappuccino is deadly for messing with your cognitive system, it lifts you up bringing you down again with a bang. It is found in chocolate, the good old cup of tea, soft drinks which are advertised. Form first hand experience I have witnessed how those taking methadone drink gallons of tea laced with three or four spoonfuls of sugar, coffee, sugary high powered drinks, while some smoke as if a funnel is sticking out through the top of their head.

Alcohol that acceptable and reliable drink, might remain your friend when you need to visit him once a week ,he can become like an obsessive lover stalking, demanding ,tormenting your every wakening moment. Then you are in the shit as you could be on the slippery road to a chemical liver, a drooping belly, headaches, mood swings, depression, bad work attendance, and a hidden host of disorders. The liver is resilient but it is not invincible, it has its limitations with toxicity, confusion, fatigue, high blood presser these can be signs of an- over stretched- liver.

Many of those on methadone also suffer from hepatitis or H.I.V. Inflammation of the liver occurs when exposure to a chemical or certain drugs, shared needles, or to a metabolic disorder. Methadone is a chemical it is not a headless corpse, it is a chemical given to methadone users and some have hepatitis or H.I, V. Can this be good practice to continually heap chemicals into an individual's whose liver may be struggling to cope with toxic overload or when methadone shall have to be administered in larger doses due to a liver working on half strength.

Metabolic disorders occur when the chemistry of the body is disturbed, an under or over active thyroid Gland can be responsible for this malfunctioning of the endocrine system which releases hormones throughout the body. That is the body's natural processes. Methadone is not a natural chemical it is a synthetic Opioid analgesic drug resembling Morphine. It does affect the body's metabolism as it induces side effects such as vomiting, dizziness, dry mouth, constipation, which in its self causes a build- up of toxicity in the body.

Metabolism is responsible for breaking down of complex substances, to be taken up and used in the body. The energy needed to keep the body functioning is the basal metabolic rate, the(BMR) increases our response to stress, fear, illness, and is controlled by hormones such as thyroxin, adrenaline, insulin(overuse of sugar), if the body experiences a malfunction in these glands it kick starts a chain reaction which affects other organs in the body.

A toxic liver cannot process toxins therefore how can they be eliminated from the body. The first line of defence is the thymus gland which lies beneath the throat, it secretes hormones to stimulate the white blood cells when the overworked liver cannot rid the body of toxins in the normal way of excretion , the only avenue out is by the blood stream, which in turn sets off the immune system to release Russell Crow look alike- gladiator cells, to protect the toxins from entering the blood stream. A war of attrition begins as the over taxed immune system struggles to stop the assault. When the body s immune system is over taxed Autoimmune disease can result in diseases like arthritis, or lupus. Hepatitis belongs to this order of disease; a reaction to certain types of drugs can be one of the symptoms which in turn are treated with corticosteroid, and immunosuppressant.

Interferon which in its self can have side effects, of depression, dizziness, vomiting, tiredness, is prescribed to treat viral infections such as autoimmune disorder. Do you get the picture? It is like a merry go round and I have left out the continuous use of the methadone dosage.

Fruit drinks contain corn syrup called fructose, dextrose is sugar extracted from cornstarch(remember starch is used in the manufacture of methadone) lactose which is in milk some people are lactose intolerant which causes an reaction in the body whenever milk is consumed. Sucrose made from cane or beet, Melrose made from starch,

Most tinned food baked beans, tinned vegetables, peas, pasta sauce, sweet and sour speaks for it-self, tomato ketchup, biscuits, cakes, bagels, raisings, dates, sweets ,chocolate, ice-cream, yogurt, artificial sweeteners contain the chemical aspartame, as deadly as a rattle snake as it is over one hundred times sweeter than its original sugar, crisp.

It is reported to affect Serotonin causing the dreaded mood swings. Honey gives you a lift because of its high sugar content, jams, grapes, and a host of other foods which release sugar rapidly into the blood stream , causing the liver to work twice as hard to counteract the hormones insulin, adrenaline and cortical, as the liver struggles to rid itself of a fat build up. Drugs, medications all impact on the over worked liver

Rapid Release

What would we do with- our sugar boost, its sweetness deceives the body into believing that all is sweetness and light The woman with hips that do a rumba without a partner will be a big sugar consumer, or a chocolate freak, who suffers the highs and drops of high sugar intake.

Sugar lurks in many foods this carbohydrate is in many a shelf life product, peas, beans, biscuits, Cakes, fizzy drinks it is sometimes under glucose, sucrose, lactose, corn syrup, honey. The list is endless

Sugar is a robber it depletes, nutrients that the liver needs in order to function. When you see a person with a big bum, large thighs, and stout belly you can be sure they are downing processed foods laced with hidden sugar dangers .because this refined carbohydrate is lurking behind every tin of peas, beans, biscuits fizzy drinks, chocolate, sweets, sauces, honey, dressing spaghetti bolognas, sweet and sour sauces all most all processed foods have some form of sugar in them. We become addicted to these sweet foods because they work on the part of the brain that deals with pleasure. Ironically it is this pleasure centre that heroin binds to causing addiction...

The more carbohydrates we eat that has rapid release, the more you need, this occurs because the body needs a balanced intake of protein, carbohydrates, minerals, vitamins, water, if you are not eating a balanced diet or eating foods that are reactive, neurotransmitters in the brain cannot produce serotonin so the cravings for more fatty sugar, chocolate, coffee junk food, is needed to trigger the release of serotonin

Slow releasing carbohydrates that are beneficial and the source of nutrition needed for normal body functioning is not refined where the vitamins and minerals are removed, but those found in foods that release blood sugar slowly into the blood stream.

The Islets of Langerhans are located in the pancreas, whenever we eat carbohydrates they set of a release of glucose, the result of which is a rush of insulin. As the intake of carbohydrates high in sugary content is not in keeping with the body's normal metabolism this false high rush has the down side of a drop starting a chain of events of carbohydrate high verses insulin drop. To keep the body homeostasis everything must be taken in moderation in accordance with what the liver, endocrine system, central nervous system, neurotransmitters nutritional requirements, that are not hidden sugar dangers

When the hormone insulin cannot convert the excess glucose an increase in weight occurs, when we indulge in stuffing sugary foods into our mouths, as a substitute for comfort, stress, anxiety, fear we can end up looking like ripened zombies with arses trailing the footpath...

Green diesel is laced with sugar to make it drinkable, when someone is drinking 80mls to 102mls a day that turns into 1,680 miles a week in a month His 3,3 60 mills multiply that by eleven and the sum is 36,520,00 Per year, that the liver must rid itself to remain functioning properly. Add to that coffee, sugary drinks, soft drinks, medication for other aliments like not sleeping, constipation ,valium, psychosis, epilepsy and a number of complaints associated with substance abuse,

Constipation is the number one complaint amongst those on methadone treatment the infrequent Bowel movements causes a blotted belly as dry impacted stools stubbornly refuse to empty itself from the bowel, the result can be lack of concentration, a feeling of fullness, and lack of appetite, or stomach cramps. This can be due to lack of fibre in the diet Some individuals live in hostels which leaves them little expectancy of cooking a gourmet meal let alone understand the difference between protein, carbohydrates, and the advantages or disadvantages of health benefits, survival is the name of their game, living from one day to another homeless hunts them like the grim reaper looking over their shoulder, this reaper can come in the disguise of a guard looking for a promotion..

Bad teeth is number three on the priory list of methadone users, I was astounded at the numbers Of beautiful young woman and men without Molars in their heads, some had lost all their teeth by the ripe old age of twenty. Others had gaps as wide at the entrance into the dail- Erin

One had his false teeth eaten by the dog as he slept One thing was certain all agreed that their Teeth had deteriorated since starting the green diesel, the dentists that services areas such as Darn dale, Coolock, Ballyfermot, Ballymun, Tallaght, must be making a fortune from the taxpayer's money.

The taxpayer's money could be better spent on research into the decaying matter of rotten teeth from a chemical that causes tooth decay in the young. These missing thirty two molars that are hard bone projections, they help to form speech and as anyone who has had to have capped or false teeth they take a while to become used to. Teeth need calcium to remain healthy, could there be a link between calcium deficient and methadone taking as is evident in the link between green diesel and osteoporosis.

Loss of bone tissue is a common complaint in those on long term methadone. This condition once considered an old peoples aliment is now afflicting many of those in their prime. It can be attributed to a number of factors especially in woman past child bearing age. Most of those I have come across are healthy young a good many years away from starting the menopause so that rules that theory out. A diet that is deficient in calcium, or hormonal disorder, and smoking can accelerated calcium loss as it is lost through urine.

Smoking is a certainty with methadone users; they do it as much as they drink coffee, or tea. Hormonal disorders can be linked to chemical changes in the body, and we see how our body functions on natural chemicals to manufacture hormones, any disruption of these chemicals either by prescribed drugs or illegal drugs upsets the body's equilibrium. We make chemical substances naturally from the many foods we eat it stands to reason that deficiency in any one of these shall contribute to the many disorders that occur.

Green Diesel is a chemical one that is taken for many years, it is pumped into those who were addicted to heroin and only contributes to the problem it is supposed to solve.

The participants who avail of methadone suggest that methadone is twice as difficult to come off. Evidence shows that normal doses of methadone can cause sudden death.

Laboratory studies have demonstrated that this green diesel inhibits cardiac potassium channels Prolonging the Q T interval.

Methadone can interact with alcohol which is a central nervous depressant, and can result in the user experiencing respiratory depression

Abuse of methadone poses a risk of overdose and death. Taking alcohol or other drugs is the main reason. Methadone is legal because of its ability to hold the patient for twenty four hours, where- as heroin must be taken every three to four hours, making it less costly, the economical factor has not gone unnoticed. Diet is completely overlooked.

Diet does play a part in maintaining a healthy metabolism, one that is balanced so that it can fulfil the functions it was made for.

Healthy Carbohydrates are essential to maintain homeostasis between the liver, glands, gallbladder, neurotransmitters, heart, and pancreas.

Carbohydrates that are sensible to eat especially for those taking methadone are ones that release energy slowly. That means no sugar, honey, white bread, biscuits, scones or jam, chocolate, tea, coffee, Soft drinks, power drinks, cola, all processed foods that contain corn syrup, glucose found in the health drink, peas, beans unless sugar free, lactose in milk, fructose, white rice only eat brown and boiled, some cereals, pasta, no cooked ham or processed packed food it contains sugar or salt

Foods that help keep the liver healthy are water, black tea, wholemeal bread, porridge vegetables, that should be eaten every day, fish salmon trout, cod, or meat mostly lean, chicken or turkey. Brown rice, oat cakes,

I have listed some of the foods below

Green corner

Green vegetables, cabbage, curly kale, lettuce, Brussels sprouts, celery, cucumber, broccoli, Chinese cabbage, courgettes, green peppers Red peppers, radishes tomatoes, , lentils, apples, apple juice, Red cabbage, chicory, fennel, onions, garlic, nuts, pumpkin seeds, walnuts, strawberries, blackberries, blueberries.

Making your own dressing can be rewarding, you can be as creative as you like as long as you use only essential fatty oil .1 refer to these as the two

If the liver is constantly finding itself having to rid itself of toxic substances it is over worked, this starts a free-fall effect in that the escaping substances head to the blood stream in their hurry to get discharged, the immune system goes into over drive sending in the first round of soldiers the white blood cells to block the invading toxins.

Hormones are flushed into the body as an army of chemicals flood the system in an attempt of correcting the balance of large intakes of sugary foods. High carbohydrates and Tran's fats

Fats Glorious Fats:

The fats that most compliment and sustain our bodies are those found in deep sea fish
Such as salmon, sardines, tuna, mackerel and eggs. I am referring to the omega twins, Fats are vital food for good mental health. Our body needs a daily intake of these fats if it is to work properly. Imbalance in omega 3 or 6 is now believed to result in depression, dyslexia, ADHD, Poor memory and Alzheimer's. New evidence gathered by science suggested that individuals who suffer with schizophrenia show low levels of essential fatty acids EFA's in blood cells. By testing 72 patients who were diagnosed with the condition of schizophrenia and a follow up of 4-5 years it was concluded that those who had schizophrenia showed lower levels of linolenic acid(Omega 3) a number of those presenting for methadone suffer from this condition. Our body makes fat cholesterol saturated and monounsaturated. We get polyunsaturated omega 3 and 6By eating foods high in this compound. We saw in the last chapter how the myelin sheath is made of phospholipids a substance which consists of a saturated and unsaturated fatty acid. These energy storage and insulating molecules are important for proper brain balance. Brain cells Consist of billions of cells that must receive the correct balanced diet one consisting of nutrients that help manufacture the phospholipids membrane surrounding the cell structure known as the Myelin sheath. In order to understand why fatty acids are important for mental health we have to look at how neurons (specialized cell) role and function. These neurons differ in size and appearance and spread like short branches called dendrites meaning branch. Neurons send impulses or messages to muscles, and glands via an extension or axon which has swellings called synaptic terminals. The gap that exists between the cell and synaptic
Terminal is the gap. Whenever an impulse moves down the axon to the terminal it causes a chemical known as a neurotransmitter. A chemical fires across the gap stimulating the nearest neuron or cell. We have sensory neurons that send impulses to the nervous system via receptors which are specialized cells in organs such as skin and joints. So we have bundles of axons belonging to hundreds or thousands of neurons (specialized cells). So our body and brain are interconnected sending electrochemical impulses to the axon via way of ion channels and pumps. The methadone takers inability to beat his or her addiction is not helped by the lack of a diet rich in amino acids, essential fatty acids vitamins, and minerals. Unsaturated fatty acid or omega 3 is

needed for brain structure the brain needs fat if it is to function properly. Receptor sites lay within the myelin sheath and as we saw these must be kept in good working condition by phospholipids as they consist of both fatty acids, omega 3 and 6.olive oil contains omega 9

Diet is on the last run of methadone ladder; methadone being first because methadone binds to the receptors for twenty four hours, unlike Heroin's three or four. The individual taking methadone needs to get the green diesel first thing every morning to keep his body homeostatic (balanced) because the methadone is as potent as heroin those taking it would suffer similar withdrawal symptoms vomiting, muscle cramps, pain, the essential minerals or vitamins almost on-existent by poor diet. A diet deficiency in amino acid can be associated with neurotransmitter dysfunction.

Prostaglandins are also needed to boost our immune system and fight disease and inflammation.

Hepatitis is inflammation of the liver a condition prevalent in some methadone users due to their heroin lifestyle.

According to the British medical association who define the treatment of hepatitis sufferers maintain that if this disorder is caused by chemicals or drugs, exposure to the substance should be stopped and in some cases detoxification. Bed rest and a nourishing diet are recommended. Abstaining from alcohol is a must. Unfortunely some methadone users don't make the connection between the two. As prostaglandins help strengthen immunity and there is a connection to fatty acids then does it not make sense that doctors who treat those on methadone ensure that the vital supplements of omega 3 and 6 plus vitamin B complex could be more beneficial given on prescription than antidepressants, or sleeping pills. Placing a methadone body on higher doses when in effect they should be coming down with proper supervision especially around nutrition does not take rocket science.. A simple capsule of fish oils, vitamins and minerals could do wonders to improve the brain power, concentration or memory recall, they can help defeat depression, not to mention bringing down expenditure of the health services for the over burdened tax payer.. The much needed brain food that is found in flax seeds, walnuts (EPA &DNA) found in a diet of salmon, mackerel, tuna, eggs, omega 6 found in sunflower, pumpkin, evening primrose, meat and dairy products.

By educating those on methadone about nutrition and the dangers of Trans-fats those deadly deep fried food such as chips, fish, nuggets, and burgers, we could perhaps do away with omega efficiency. Mr Ronald mc Donnell could do his bit by way of introducing healthy food at his fast food outlets.

Like a pump house our body needs the correct components in the form of food to keep it and the brain functioning and balanced. Ion channels are protein molecules. These protein structures regulate the flow of ions, sodium, potassium, calcium, chloride. Impulses can travel at speeds of 200 miles an hour. This speed can however be effected by the myelin sheath which consists of gliad cells that wrap themselves around the axon; its insulating function allows the nerve impulses to pass from gap to gap.

When someone suffers from multiple- sucrose's it means that their body is destroying its own myelin.

Neurotransmitters jump to receptor sites and lock into one another like a jigsaw, when locked some have an excitatory effect while others are inhibitory, that decrease the timing potential of a certain neurotransmitter.

Depression which is treated with antidepressant drugs and work by depressing the central nervous system, sleeping pills, tranquillizers, cough medicine, solvents, aerosols, valium, paint, glue, alcohol, methadone, heroin, opium. All are used to reduce anxiety by blocking certain receptor sites, these medications either keep certain neurotransmitters like serotonin (depression is believed to be caused by low levels of this neurotransmitter in the body inhabiting the destruction or re-uptake of the chemical. We have over *70* different neurotransmitters which have different uses in the body due to different receptor molecules. Acetylcholine has a duel function both inhibitory and excitatory depending on the type of receiving neuron. Those with Alzheimer's disease are reported to have a deficiency of acetylcholine. Drugs known as acetylcholine erase inhibitors, Donepezil, Rivastigmine, or Glantamine block the action of the enzyme raising the level of acetylcholine increasing alertness for the suffer of Alzheimer's. Side effects are urinary difficulties, nausea, vomiting, and diarrhoea. It is also reported that these drugs can increase the risk of convulsions in some people. Heroin works in a similar fashion it locks onto neuron-receptors in the brain. Opiates can do this because they are similar in molecular shape to endorphins giving pleasurable sensations. We all have natural pain neurotransmitters but heroin abuse can deplete it leaving the body consuming more and more to fill empty receptor sites.

Methadone works or the same premise, it is highly addictive as many of those taking methadone shall confirm. It is described thus, a synthetic drug belonging to the opioid analgesic family used in severe pain, in terminal illness, to replace morphine or heroin dependence. A dose use for dependents can be fatal for a non- user. Its growing popularity in society and especially the medical profession who see it as having less destructive physical effects as heroin. It interacts with MAOIs (monoamine oxidase inhibitors) such as moclobemide, Phenelzine, Isocarboxaxid, all antidepressants and given to those who suffer from depression, phobias, or anxiety. Taken with methadone these drugs may cause a dangerous rise or fall in blood pressure. Alcohol is also forbidden while on methadone as it increases the sedative effects of the drug and may depress breathing. Overdose rating is high as is the dependence rating for this opioid analgesic.

Clinically anxiety arises when the balance of certain chemicals in the brain is disturbed, to counteract these feelings of breathlessness, shaking, palpitations, headache anti- depressants such as anxiolytics or tranquillizers are prescribed. These are also given in a hospital setting to calm or relax patients. Know as beta blockers, or benzodiazepines or benzo's to methadone users, these have a strong sedative effect especially for those suffering from insomnia a common complaint in those taking methadone.

These brand names are Alprozolam, Diazepam, Loraxepam, and Oxaxepam. Beta blockers are Atenolol, Bisoprolol, and Oxprenolol. All of these drugs carry risks with both psychological and physical dependence. When stopped suddenly they can result in symptoms such as excessive anxiety, nightmares. They should not be used with methadone or alcohol they all have a sedative effect on the central nervous system.

Methadone is acceptable in today's society, could it be because society is not subjected to handbag snatching, robbery or A. I. D.s As more research is carried out on methadone we shall no doubt see a host of health issues most of which is a result of the sugar content and the methadone user's, lack of fundamental knowledge concerning this drug which in turn is turning out a new generation of new addictive individuals.

Brain Cells:

According to the department of biological sciences our cells consist of lipids, proteins and Carbohydrates all functioning in the cell membrane.

Lipids serve many functions in organisms and are the main components of waxes pigments, steroid hormones and cell membranes.

1. Fats, steroids and phospholipids are important for the body and brain to function properly.

Fats are needed for energy storage and help insulate molecules. Phospholipids contain two fatty Acid. They serve a major function by surrounding the cell, Myelin insulates nerve fibres containing 18% protein and 76% lipid cells need to communicate with each other. Proteins are composed of amino acids. Proteins determine most of the specific functions of the membrane, over 50 have been found in red blood cells.

2. Phospholipids also manufactures the brains memory transmitter acetylcholine a deficiency in this neurotransmitter is responsible for disinterest in helping to change your circumstances and I often hear this term banded towards those on methadone.

Lack of motivation, attachment, ambivalence, is terms misunderstood when it comes to those taking drugs. First and foremost people change because they want to, or the penny drops that their drug lifestyle is slowly killing them. The methadone user attends the programme with the intention of turning his or her life around. Green diesel appears to offer this opportunity and some do come down slowly, but most on this drug do complain of great difficulty and symptoms similar to heroin withdrawal, strength is something they need in abundance. Are we searching in the wrong area if phospholipids help manufacture acetylcholine which is now believed to contain certain fatty acids, it may be of interest to research the eating habits of those on methadone for a deficiency in acetylcholine could go a long way in explaining why some can show signs of lack of motivation.

Bad memory recall is second on the methadone users list and again linked to a lack of the neurotransmitter acetylcholine. Depression follows hot in pursuit; the enormity of this condition on society conjures up images of a society heading towards a life style of antidepressant drugs. Such as SSRIs, MAOIs, TCAs, most of these cause drowsiness, dry mouth blurred vision. Eating foods rich in essential fatty acids does help to counteract depression, infections, fatigue, and cancer. A diet rich in omega 3 and 6 can help the methadone user to counteract these symptoms. It is more pleasant to walk around a supermarket shopping than to sit in a stuffy doctors waiting room waiting for a hand out of drugs that send you to never land and instil the negative emotion of being sick If we eat the incorrect foods, ones depleted in the essential fats, amino acids, complex carbohydrates then we are walking a thin line to inflicting anxiety, depression, behavioural problems, insomnia, all symptoms. I witness each day in clients on daily doses of green diesel how they must struggle with the above symptoms, unaware that their own health does lay with a diet that contains both omega 3 and 6, which can be found in polyunsaturated oils.

Most of the food consumed daily by methadone users are trans fats such are fries, crisps, burgers, chicken nuggets, deep fried, high in refined carbohydrates, processed foods, fizzy drinks all high in sugar content. Most processed foods are deficient in the important vitamins and minerals needed to make glucose into energy, amino acids into neurotransmitters, essential fats into (GLA) or (DHA) prostaglandins.

It appears that most of us are hooked on processed foods; convenience foods are devoid of this natural brain food and are laced with sugar, refined Carbohydrates and are starving our own body and brain of the most important nutrients needed for mental health.

We are failing to rebuild the hormones, and neurotransmitters that keep our brain ticking over smoothly. We are in essence causing the many mental illness that afflicts society not to mention providing the large profit margins to the drug companies. Those on methadone are ingesting daily intakes of opium, this close relative lures receptor sites its sole function is its life span of twenty four hours that its user can go with their next fix. As we have already read opium taken over a long duration can leaves the body's .natural chemicals redundant.

Methadone must be sweetened in order for the taker to consume it. In order for sugar to be used for human consumption the sugar cane must be processed. It is this processing method that depletes this commodity of 90% of the vitamins and minerals needed by the human body. If this is so then we are receiving no benefit from lacing an already dangerous chemical with one that sends our sugar blood levels through the roof. Could it also be said that we as a society deem it appropriate to feed this green monster to clients who are oblivious to its dangers. Sugar as we have already discussed sends insulin levels into overdrive as it struggles to deal with the onslaught of a high energy intake. Not only is it causing adrenaline glands to over perform it also has an effect on the neurotransmitter needed to deal with stressful situations, the liver that power house of the body is also effected as it works feverish to store the excesses glycogen. Refined carbohydrates such as sugar can cause a glucose imbalance leading to symptoms such as insomnia, lack of concentration, fatigue, depression all complaints associated with most of those on methadone. Refined carbohydrates are like drugs the more that you ingest the more the body craves. It is as if the body craves the very foods that damage it. Our body needs carbohydrates because cells membranes are made from both protein and carbohydrates but what the brain and body does not need is refined carbohydrates that does nothing but erode the vitamins or minerals it needs to maintain good mental health.

Evidence now shows that children who consume foods with high sugar content, or who are fed a diet of deep fried chips, nuggets, fried food, suffer from concentration problems, memory recall and aggressive behaviour. Most children today skip breakfast grabbing crisps or muffins on their way to school. Some schools have provided breakfast for children who come from economical deprived communities but most of the food consumed is refined. Carbohydrates such as white bread, processed cereal, fruit drinks processed with sugar.

Adrenalin is the hormone most affected by high consumptions of sugar; adrenalin is needed in times of stress. If some children are consuming foods high in sugar they become anxious as sugar levels fall leading to tiredness, and lack of concentration, Soft drinks especially power drinks are now doing the rounds as advertising firms swap up famous celebrities to promote these drinks as the new energy giver. What the label on most of these drinks fail to express is that while sugar does give an instant energy high, it is like a balloon what goes up, must come down so when sugar levels drop or when little Tom or Mary throws a temper tantrums, could it be a result of the aggression association with sugar withdrawal.

The foods we consume needs to be cooked before we eat it and so foods that are processed like chicken wings, nuggets, burgers, chips have the added result of over exposure to the destruction of the complex carbohydrates needed to fuel little Tom to Mary's brain. When children are hyperactive at bedtime it could be down to your feeding methods. The person on methadone, who only eats junk food plus a diet of refined carbohydrates laced with sugar, or salt, is oblivious to the daily damage they may be doing to their health.

Those on methadone should be given the choice to change their eating habits by way of education. Knowledge about the goodness of eating fruit on a daily basis, a handful of blueberries topped on hot porridge, or a slice of wholegrain bread with a poached egg shall do more to enhance the readiness of their body and brain to the stressful situations that most of this consuming methadone must confront daily. To educate methadone users about dietary habits is to fuel better mental health and children who receive a healthy diet of balanced food that feed their neurotransmitters the correct nutrition, one fuelled by vitamins and minerals and amino acids. Breakfast is an important start for everyone's day but especially so for methadone users. It does not take rocket science to see most individuals on the program don't eat breakfast they arrive at the centre with perhaps only a few chocolate bars to sustain them until they leave. Bad eating habits impair the brains function depleting certain neurotransmitters from working properly. Poor concentration, bad memory recall, go to together like peaches and cream for those on methadone as does lack of motivation. Most report they have difficulty in coming down from the green diesel that blocks certain receptor sites. Methadone does not fuel the brain; its sugar content stifles and stops the brain from seeking a complete and proper balance needed to stop the many mental health issues that some methadone users experience. Until those in the medical profession take the appropriate care and attention to the diet of these on methadone we shall see a society strung out on refined food, sugar, antidepressants, stimulants, nicotine, coffee, trans fats, and chocolate all food now medically known to interfere with the bodies neurotransmitters causing long term effects such as depression, anxiety and stress.

Brain pollution:

Our bodies are made up of neurotransmitter and hormones which are released by glands such as the thyroid adrenal, pituitary and sex glands. It keeps all of these in working order with methylamine.

It is this compound that produces phospholipids needed to keep the brain and body in a healthy state. They also play a role in cell function whenever someone has a child with Down syndrome it can be established they have a low methylamine level. Scientists now believe this also plays apart in many conditions such as depression and memory loss. Some of these mental conditions can be associated with high homocysteine levels that we get when we consume a diet depleted in a balance of vitamin B especially as this important vitamin helps manufacture the enzymes needed for the conversion of homocysteine into glutamine. If we are eating foods lacking the family of B vitamins and folic acid we can face a build up of these dangerous toxins which can leave us with high homocysteine blood levels. Those on methadone or who suffer from depression can and should have their levels of homocysteine measured by a blood test,

It is now known that individuals who suffer from the disorder of schizophrenia have high levels of homocysteine. A normal level is 7, anything over that needs to be looked at. The higher your homocysteine levels the more likely you are to suffer from a default in methylation. The food we eat can play a vital role in raising levels. In an earlier chapter on neurotransmitters we saw how these mental chemicals can either be reprocessed (reuptake) or are destroyed by enzymes. Enzymes are important as they depend on nutrient. This is where vitamins are important if we are to lower the toxic homocysteine levels for better mental health. The B complex vitamins are important as is folic acid and zinc; homocysteine is a protein which we get from the food we consume. Nutrients rich in B6 and B12 and folic acid are now seen as improving mental health.

A diet of eggs, wholegrain, spinach, meat and milk, has vitamin B2. Bananas and wholegrain Bread will provide B6, meat and eggs will provide B12 while folic acid can be got from green leafy vegetables. Zinc you shall get from eating nuts, sunflower seeds and fish. As most individuals lack a proper intake of these important minerals and Vitamins a supplement of these important methtylation building nutrients would be beneficial to methadone users. Most Methadone users consume large amounts of coffee, smoke and live in stressful conditions. Most are dependent on social Welfare, live in cramped family conditions where aggression can visit them on a daily basis.

Most struggle to cope and have abused heroin their drug of choice for many years leaving them deprived of family, homeless or worse. Stress strides beside them threatening to overpower them due to a lack of coping skills, when we attend at our doctor with stress we usually leave with a script for more medication. Doctors are dealers of legal drugs; it is how we medically train them.

Everything is built on theory, all medical symptoms are treated with similar medication, and mental illness is defined to a set of concepts and behaviours and treated as such.

Any doctor worth his or her salt will treat their patients as individuals, keeping an open mind but above all listening to the patient and not act like the hair dresser giving you the style they believe that best suits you while over looking what you ask for.

Findings now suggest that high copper levels deplete manganese and zinc the two minerals that are vital to those suffering from psychotic states, if this evidence is already out there why is it not taken up and explored by those prescribing Methadone.

Insomnia is also a common occurrence associated with individuals on methadone it can also be attributed to depleted Minerals such as manganese, we need sleep to heal our bodies, and deprivation of sleep can create a host of conditions, when we spend a sleepless night we behave like a bull with a massive hangover. Until we explore all avenues to generate a better understanding of why those taking methadone suffer the horrors of not sleeping only then can we get the best possible results for those who cannot communicate their needs and fears but bury them in a haze of drugs as thick as a fog down a mine.

The hand that holds the pen and which at times can be too rapid to write a prescription for another drug to someone who could benefit from a simple mineral and vitamin test is not giving due attention to many underlying factors associated with addiction.

We have a string of issues that we cannot afford to place on the long finger or keep feeding the economical machine that is the pharmaceutical companies when that money could be better spent at looking at certain deficiency in those who present with methadone or other addictions"

"Could it be safe to say the humble pineapple or banana a day could keep the drug companies at bay"?

As I listen to continual complaints from those taking this thick green diesel as to why they feel depressed or lack motivation I witnesses a growing generation hooked on a cousin of heroin they complain of how some doctors refuse to listen, or play god with their bodies, I ponder at how we have reached this situation.

Some of the most serious complaints are those where the doctor refuses to allow choice or discussion about when they can come down on vie, making the choice of writing a prescription to accompany methadone, sleeplessness is cured by another pill, a pill also as addictive as the one keeping them awake.

Zinc deficiency does damage your health it is critical for mental health. A deficient associated with schizophrenia a mental disorder that requires strong drugs, as does anxiety, depression which can be symptoms associated with long term drug taking.

Other symptoms like hyperactivity, ADHD, dyslexia can be found in children of those who have abused drugs could it be the depletion of minerals such as zinc, magnesium, have a link to these disorders. Hormone imbalance associated with the endocrine system the main hormone making machine which must receive a balanced diet if it is to function properly, we do not have enough research on the effects that this potent drug may have on hormone disturbance. Stress also depletes zinc as does infections which many methadone users suffer from, hepatitis being the most common. A handful of nuts or a diet rich in fish could not only counteract these deficiencies but could help cut the Government bill while reducing the huge percentages paid to the manufactures who profit from making methadone. Something as simple as eating nuts, sunflower seeds, lentil soup wholegrain bread or supplementing vitamin B1 to improve concentration B3 to help counteract psychosis and depression, vitamin B5 for stress, vitamin B6 for poor memory folic acid for depression, psychosis or anxiety, a vitamin C tablet shall help dispel all depression, bad appetite and loss of motivation. By eating a daily diet of green vegetables, bananas, eggs, fruit, nuts, pineapple, sunflower seeds and cutting out processed foods, white refined sugar, bread, crisps, fizzy drinks, high performance drinks, fried food, deep fried chips, nuggets you can improve not only your mental ability and intellect but your overall well being

Alongside them each day stress, smoking' all accompanies high homocysteine levels, perhaps doctors are adverting their gaze in the wrong direction in order to stop neurotransmitter pollution we should examine homocystenie as a way of helping those on methadone to maximise good mental health.

Trans fats damage your health that is a warning you shall not encounter on the vast variety of processed foods or oils, nor shall the man deep frying your fish and chips as you taste buds drip saliva from the side of your mouth explain to you the dangers of eating trans fats or rubbish fast food. Not only is he frying your food but he is helping you to fry your brain. In an earlier chapter we discovered how our brain is made up of 60 % fat these are not the bad Trans greasy fats associated with the smell of half cooked rashers or egg. The Sunday fry or chips dished up following a night on the tills of drinking. Trans fats contain Hydrogenated oils, these dangerous trans fats are mostly found in underprivileged areas because not only is the chipper a must one or two nights a week, followed by takeaways and fast food outlets that shall remain nameless but are popular with children. Visit any supermarket and the Trans fat foods are situated in a location best geared for breaking your psychological willpower. You need all your strength to pass as neurotransmitters scream that you need a quick fix of refined crabs, chocolate or jelly babies full of starch or sugar. Less cooking bang them on the pan and grab that much needed rest from to- day's stress.

These dangerous Trans fats enter the body quickly, tricking your mental process. They also block serotonin from reaching the Brain. The important prostaglandins and omega 3 and 6 are diverted from their important role of feeding the brain. Smoking also depletes zinc which is important for the production of serotonin and anyone that works in a drug program will know how hooked many methadone users have become on fags.

Smoking is another dangerous past time not only is it responsible for zinc depleation, lung cancer, heart disease, but is now know to latch unto serotonin receptors, while giving you a cough like an old man of eighty. You are what you eat, you are also what you smoke so if you become depressed, suffer with anxiety you are damaging your own health in essence you are frying your brain, and giving your lungs a blasting they can do without. If you want to smoke you can make sure you are getting foods such as carrots, peppers, berries; black berries are good fruit such as lemons. Tuna, nuts, spinach, sardines, mackerel those foods contain the antioxidants, which help to destroy free radicals.

Listening to your brain

As stated in the previous chapter those on methadone can do a lot for their depression, mood swings, and bad memory, poor concentration by looking at their diet, doctors who prescribe methadone can also enhance the lives of the people they serve by studying addiction or drug dependency from the angle of diet. While drug abuse is perceived from both the disease and psychological model. A doctor worth his salt would enquire into the client's daily diet. Most of those that have a dependency on opiates, come from economical deprived backgrounds Diet takes a back seat to survival. The body needs protein which is not found in a greasy burger or refined white bread stuffed with chips or crisps. In underprivileged social areas amino acids could be perceived as something that you steer clear off. The acid they encounter gives you a high.

Our body needs protein to regenerate our cells, neurotransmitters are messages that the brain sends to our hormones, which in turn are released into the blood stream. Adrenal is one such hormone which is released in stressful situations. Those who take heroin and methadone do so to elevate stress as this cousin of morphine blocks out everything connected with fear, stress all problems are sent to join the foreign legion once the green diesel is ingested. Could it be then that those on long term methadone use suffer a deficiency in the building blocks of the brain amino acids? Most methadone users I have encountered have shown symptoms of depression, some suffer with psychosis. Most have an insufficient diet of white bread, biscuits, processed sugary foods, red bull, alcohol, fried food and powered drinks, a combination for disaster a bomb waiting to explode, as they struggle to come down off green diesel. The blame game is played out in earnest as Molly must become an accomplice in the road of survival. Most of those taking methadone are seen by society as lacking in motivation, not wanting to do anything about their circumstances, could the medical profession be barking up the wrong tree by insisting that those taking drugs of abuse are lay-a-bouts, are unwilling to take control of their lives.

It is now common knowledge especially with recent research that deficiency in amino acids can cause lack of motivation, depression, apathy, bad concentration and bad memory recall. Tryptophan which belongs to the amino acid family can promote and enhance a feel good factor in those who suffer from the above symptoms. Scientics research shows that they have identified over 54 neurotransmitters in our bodies, and are discovering more every day. As humans we are a bundle of chemicals it stands to reason that whatever we pump into our bodies shall have a direct reaction. If we feed ourselves a cocktail of bad food, alcohol, drugs prescribed or illegal then the brain does not have to manufacture the neurotransmitters naturally .It becomes redundant ,as the body relays on its daily dose of methadone or manmade drugs.

Recycling:

Amino acid is the mainstay of neurotransmitters which are chemical messages that are electrical impulses which move down the axon to the synaptic gap. Once released these are received at the receptor sites before reuptake where the chemical is reabsorbed for further use. This continuous supply of amino acids we receive by way of food therefore we need these important essential amino acids to maintain a healthy state of mind. Serotonin is the neurotransmitter that helps to maintain mood and emotion and appetite. Certain carbohydrates especially white bread, or pasta are reported to deplete serotonin as the body needs to work twice as hard to raise serotonin levels to the brain, when someone presents with depression it is believed they suffer from low serotonin levels. Individuals who suffer from depression are prescribed anti- depressants which work by blocking serotonin from being reabsorbed allowing the chemical to remain at the synapses for a longer period. Selective serotonin re-uptake inhibitors know as (SSRIs) these drugs increase the levels of neurotransmitters by blocking their reabsorption.

MOAIs act by stopping the breakdown of the neurotransmitters (natural chemicals) serotonin, and norepinephrine.

While this does relieve the unhappiness and low mood associated with low serotonin levels antidepressants can build up in the liver resulting in a lump of flab that is resistance to come off your midriff. Because serotonin is associated with the area of the brain which controls eating weight gain usually occurs. Foods rich in tryptophan are a more suitable suggestion that can raise serotonin levels. Some doctors prescribe antidepressants like smarties and it is common knowledge that some individuals on methadone also receive antidepressants, or sleeping pills, top this with alcohol and you have a recipe for disaster, a good doctor will know his or her stuff and ask their patient "what is your daily diet" they shall have read and learned how important daily protein and complex carbohydrates are for a healthy mental state. They shall take time to explore what amount of amino acids, essential fatty acids, are consumed by those under their care. They should know neurotransmitters are made from amino acids and a diet rich in protein, vegetables, minerals, and vitamins especially the B complex family for the nervous system, is essential for good mental health.

How important is it for those on methadone to include protein in their diet? (Essential)

Amino acids are essential to avoid neurotransmitter deficiencies. Remember that heroin which many methadone users abused can deplete the natural chemicals needed by the body for healthy functioning. Breakfast is a must for those on methadone especially porridge and stewed apple which not only releases sugar slowly into the blood stream but sets the methadone taker up with a head start on a healthier way of eating. Lunch can consist of tuna and leafy green vegetables on a bed of lentils. A platter of salmon or tin of tuna with bread beans or a helping of broccoli will maintain a good helping of protein and in time enhance neurotransmitters helping to build the amino acids essential for good mental health. It is difficult to believe in the year 2009 some of those I work with and who are on daily intake of methadone eat a diet of eight chocolate bars, buns, and lives in a homeless hostel. Governments spend millions each year maintaining methadone programs when surely we can give vitamins and minerals, information and advice on how neurotransmitter deficiencies can result in depression, mood swings, confusion and lifetime of other mental illness. A daily intake of foods with the appropriate essential amino acids that is needed for good brain power has been neglected as Pharmaceuticals companies make big bucks from the growing dependency on methadone. The lentil soup that granny made was of more substance than processed or deep fried foods. Granny knew her stuff; she was fuelling your brain. The new kid on the block that can ensure you are keeping depression at bay can be taken by adding a small amount of protein power over the bowl of porridge. Of course like all things balance is the key word, everything in moderation. If we consume large amounts of amino acids our body sucks up bone calcium. Osteoporosis or brittle bones a disease that is on the increase and one associated with methadone use can be attributed to high protein intake could this be the result of dairy products such as hard cheeses which is now the thing we put in sandwiches or is it something in the methadone itself.

As children we were fed breast milk which has glutamine an amino acid, tomatoes also contain glutamine that helps heal our gut. Those on methadone would benefit from tomatoes soup natural made from organic tomatoes as it contributes to strengthening the immune system it is common knowledge that most of those who abused drugs have the virus or hepatitis, a diet high in vitamins can help

GABA the neurotransmitter associated with de-stressing us can be found in glutamine it does this by controlling the release of the hormone adrenal. Adrenaline is released when we become stressed or anxious, most individuals who partake of methadone live stressful lives or as granny would say they "live on their nerves". Perhaps that organic tomato grown in the back garden the one you could smell its sweetness was of more benefit than we released. As we have read in a previous chapter we need acetylcholine for memory. A form of glutamate *is* now studied in an effort to establish how people with an increase in this neurotransmitter are more mentally alert and have good memory recall this amino acid can be found in fish, vegetables, and some dairy products. In order to beat depression and enhance motivation those on methadone could improve their mental health by receiving, food rich in protein, eating vegetables, beans, and lentils. Fish, tomatoes, turkey, lean meat only and not as often as every day meat can be replaced with fish or Lentils, and a platter of green vegetables.

Remember most commercial food products use hydrolyzed vegetable proteins as flavouring agents, monosodium glutamate is a flavour enhancer it is a sodium salt of glutamic acid that is found in fermented soy products, which is done by hydrolyzing the bean and wheat protein by fugal fermentation. This type of produce can cause food intolerance in many people. The receptors for human sense of taste are located on the tongue and the soft palate. They respond to sweet, (sugar) sour (like lemon juice) bitter (strong coffee) salt (salt) (monosodium glutamate, savouries, crisps)

Flavour molecules enter the air in the nose where they are detected by millions of receptors (specialized cells) this feeds information to the brain. The back of the nose respond to thousands of chemicals in food. Flavouring is added by manufactures to food products to give, enhance or intensify flavour.

Smell is also a factor in many of those who relapse back to heroin use; our senses play an important role determining what foods we eat. The flavour of food results from the stimulation of the chemical senses of taste and smell these are carried out in the taste buds. There are over 1,200 compounds of food additives available in commercial foods. Natural flavouring comes from natural plants, herbs, spices, animals or microbial fermentations. Artificial flavourings are mixtures of synthetic compounds these are more commonly used to flavour self =life foods due to the cost, and the lack of natural ones. Seaweed is an amino acid and is added to soup; other compounds added are riboncleotides, guanosine monophosphate, yeast extract, or vegetable proteins .soups, gravies, sauces, canned and frozen vegetables and cooked meats.

Some of these can cause food intolerance of allergies. Those on methadone need to become aware of the interaction between chemicals in food.

Help yourself

Many individuals on methadone do suffer with hepatitis, this disease of the liver shall have occurred due to long term use of heroin and sharing of dirty needles, or unprotected sex. Some shall have to undergo a course of interferon in a bid to correct any damage to the liver. This form of chemotherapy is given by injection its side effects include depression, loss of hair, weight loss, tiredness. Cytokines, interferon Alfa and interleukin-2 stimulate the immune system to attack certain cancers. Unpleasant side effects can be helped by counselling support from friends and family, antidepressant drugs cannot be taken by the methadone taker therefore it is important that the family of B complex vitamins be taken to keep depression at bay. It should be common knowledge among doctors that this group of handy vitamins can help the methadone taken to maintain a healthy mental attitude as they undergo this treatment. Many of those who have abused heroin for long periods or have abused alcohol can become deficient in the group of B vitamins.

Because B vitamins can help the nervous system and as these can be dispelled rapidly from the body they need to be taken daily or given by injection weekly. B1 vitamin helps glucose which the brain needs to make energy. It also improves concentration and the creative processes helping individual to think almost on their feet, niacin or B3 vitamins is a must if someone on methadone is to remain mentally alert Some methadone users are known to suffer with eczema skin disorder that results from an allergy to perfumes, sticking plasters, cats and dogs,plants,drugs,nickel. This condition causes dry itching rash than can blister. Cold tar is used while corticosteroid creams or ointments relieve the inflammation.

One tablet of B3 (niacin) is reported to combat this disorder and recent research indicates that it is also valuable in those suffering from psychosis or schizophrenia, It can improve memory and help keep dementia at bay. This vitamin is also helpful with those suffering with cognitive disorders. One of the clients who underwent interferon was put on the vitamin B complex and had no side effects such as depression associated with interferon, perhaps doctors could explore the possibilities of a daily dose of niacin B3 to methadone users. The clients I work with a percentage would have been diagnosed with schizophrenia niacin B3 is reported to show good results for those who suffer from this disorder.

Acetylcholine neurotransmitters help us to deal with stress as most methadone users live their lives enduring stressful situations and as methadone depletes motivational skills vitamin B5 can enhance the release of acetylcholine.

Most individuals who abuse drugs for years or who abuse alcohol, have a deficiency in the B complex family, this vitamin can be found in sardines or the good old eggs yoke are a rich source of vitamin B5. Eggs and fish especially sardines contain phosphate chlorine which in turn is essential for keeping memory decline at bay. Another source of this source rich phosphate chlorine is lecithin. Fat build up is a common complaint from those on methadone especially as it accumulates around the middle leaving many of those using it with a thick tyre like belly beneath thin jumpers or jeans they find great difficulty puncturing.

This build up of midriff fat is a devil to shift and leaves some to carry added weight like a lost twin around with them.

one of the important vitamins for those taking methadone is B12, B6 and folic acid this combination work in harmony with BC (niacin) to enhance the neurotransmitters. If we are deficient in any of those we can suffer from a fuzzy thinking process, confusion, unable to think straight. Serotonin deficiency can lead to depression if someone is lacking in the vitamin B6they shall not have the normal serotonin. B6 is also linked to helping us deal with stress. Some individuals on methadone will suffer from H.I.V therefore B6 can help them deal with the daily stress associated with the knowledge of having this disease, research carried out on patients suffering with schizophrenia or depression showed an improvement when given vitamin B6 and folic acid. I personally saw great improvement in my well being after taking folic acid due to depletion associated with an under active thyroid.

DR. M. Carney makes the suggestion that folic Acid and vitamin B12 deficiency can result in patients suffering from mental health disorders vitamin B6, B12 and folic acid deficiency should be considered when those on methadone complain with symptoms of depression this may be a better option than anti-depressants heaped as an already over worked liver one that may already be damaged from H.I.V and hepatitis. The good old

orange tablet that ma dropped into water the one that fascinated you as a child as it fizzed in the glass also had benefits not only does it starve off the yearly flu symptoms but it helps balance its important function in the brain as it works in tandem with neurotransmitters helping to reduce depression and schizophrenia the indication being that those who suffer vitamin E deficiency or schizophrenia need more of this vitamin than those who do not suffer from the disorder. I may be a worthwhile exercise for those doctors who prescribe methadone to have a vitamin and mineral count done before prescribing anti-depressants. Most of those on methadone or heroin report muscle cramp especially when withdrawing from this potent opium. Muscle cramps now associated with magnesium deficiencies perhaps supplementing this mineral could not only improve withdrawal from methadone but improve the nervous reaction and irritability that most individuals experience when coming down off green diesel. Calcium also has a role to play as it clams the nervous system and helps strengthen bones this once common disease associated with older people is rampant among those on high doses of methadone.

Both calcium and magnesium contribute to dispelling suicidal intentions depression and insomnia which is a common complaint from those I work with and who have been prescribed methadone.

When they complain to their doctor the response is another prescribed drug (a sleeping pill), magnesium is a mineral and has become depleted due to of chemicals such as pesticides and fungicides.

Could it be that opium such as heroin and methadone work in a similar manner as psychoactive drugs they deplete the levels of both calcium and magnesium. Or could it be the amount of protein based substances used in the processing of foods, substances such as sallcylate or amine that is now know to cause food intolerance. Recent reports suggest that a high intake of protein can result in bone loss. As most of the food consumed by those taking green diesel is mainly of deep fried and processed food they lack the most important compound that turns vegetables green (chlorophyll molecules). Sunflower seeds, pumpkin seeds and nuts all contain this compound vital to fight off depression.

It is a well known fact that suicide is high amongst those taking methadone while I acknowledge that some duel drug and this can be a factor, it fails to explain why when methadone is available and plentiful we are still experience hype in suicidal tendencies of those on steady doses of this green diesel. Why do doctors who prescribe this concoction not question its reaction on the already depleted most vital minerals and vitamins that are needed for good mental health. Doctors need to examine the deficiency of the mineral manganese and zinc that is crucial for the production of stress hormones, immune function and the pancreas and helps with the production of insulin, bones liver and kidneys. This mineral contributes to burning fat; the role of fat lingering at the methadone user's middle could mean there is a deficiency. Your increase in appetite where you are always hungry and forever raiding the fridge could be the result of a lack of leptin also associated with a diet lacking zinc. Another reason those on methadone need this mineral is the chronic stressful situations in their daily lives zinc helps to control cortisol levels ensuring this hormone is in plentiful supply. It is found in natural fruits like bananas and pineapple. Could these simple fruits help to counteract the imbalance of these minerals that most of those who suffer from schizophrenia are now thought to have a deficiency in manganese, while a lack of vitamin B3 can contribute to helping those with mental problems such as bio-polar.

We live in a world of chemicals our food is drowned in chemicals, most houses still have copper pipes that delivers drinking water, legal drugs are awash with- in communities, our food is saturated with herbicides, fungicides, flavouring, antidepressants, uppers downers, unless we address the growing concerns of treating some forms of depression with drugs as addictive as heroin or methadone we shall have a crisis on our hands.

Best buddies

Phospholipids help to make the memory neurotransmitter acetylcholine they also help nutrients which are needed to process methylation. These are vital in keeping the body's chemicals and neurotransmitters functioning in a balanced way. According to Patrick Helford(2007) phospholipids are the brains best buddy as they protect against Alzheimer's disease. The phospholipids responsible for this are chlorine, homocyoteine, and phosphatidyl serine. Patrick Halfords makes the startling discovery that we need to provide our brain with chlorine a nutrients essential for good memory, as loss in memory can be attributed to a lack of depleted chlorine. Because our memory transmitter acetylcholine is made from chlorine, whenever there is deficiency it can result in memory loss.

Chorine is essential to combat homocysteine, those suffering with Alzheimer's disease appear to show higher blood levels of homocysteine. Following a complex series of conversionshomocysteine becomes a virtual brain nutrient (S.A.M.E). Phosphatidyl serine helps memory, learning, vocabulary skills, and concentration, sociability which can be measured as lacking in those with the condition schizophrenia. What I find interesting about Holfort's findings is the connection he makes between nutritional deficiencies and depressive symptoms, which are prevalent in those on large intakes of methadone. Because (PS) has the ability to enhance brain cell communication, as it is linked to receptor sites and like schizophrenia it is the failure of reuptake of the neurotransmitter dopamine that causes the disorder. Another vital component in the phospholipids family is (DMAE) found in sardines, this ensures a smooth supply of acetylcholine into the blood stream which in turn feeds the brain. Eggs and sardines are a good source of phospholipids. Essential fats are what help fuel the brain and body without which we may suffer a deficiency in important brain function as stated I witness first hand. These fats (not hard fats) can improve concentration while memory is sharpened in some who have abused drugs for long periods. Essential fatty acids have helped bring down my high cholesterol that resulted from an under- active thyroid and poor metabolism. Now I can eat three eggs a week without any problems. Egg whites contain peptides needed for the conversion of protein into amino acid.

The dried granules lecithin is also high in phospholipids it helps with our cognitive system. I usually sprinkle a large tablespoon over my porridge each morning or mix it with flaxseed oil and sprinkle it over baby spinach leaves, it also helps with fat deposits especially those which linger or outstay their welcome on my hips. A piece of liver (lambs) or wholegrain bread with a slight covering of peanut butter is a great way to maintain that the myelin sheath is insulated. By eating a diet balanced with complex carbohydrates, protein, fruit and vegetables we can help boost our brain power, beat depression, memory loss and mood.

A Bundle of Chemicals:

Allergies are common in people on methadone and one I believe warrants investigation. New research suggests that allergies and addiction are one and the same. Interesting findings considering that when methadone or alcohol is stopped the body goes into withdrawal, craving the very substance that is damaging it. Certain foods cause an allergic reaction, we know that food gives us a feeling of satisfaction, refined carbohydrates release serotonin the neurotransmitter responsible for mood, and appetite, an overload of these starchy foods can result in a high of satisfaction of fullness, comfort,, happiness, that is until serotonin levels drop leaving a craving for the very foods, biscuits, crisps, trans fats, bread, that your body needs to remain homeostatic. (Remember most of these foods are laced with food flavourings, sugar and salt) so the person consuming large amounts of processed foods can find that the hidden sugar content has sent their insulin levels rocketing only to drop with a wallop, as their adrenal glands rush to accommodate its neighbour gland.

What is also overlooked is the role amines (amino acids) have in all of this. Amines can have a biological function which is diverse; they can be beneficial or harmful. These are found in over 70% of foods such as meat, fish, chocolate, cheeses, and gluten like substances wheat, barley, oats, and rye.

Amines are described as biogenic such as (serotonin, cadaverine, and histamine) the latter is linked with an allergy to pollen, and conjunctivitis.

According to a European project (May2002) that carried out research on biogenic amines these can be detrimental as they cause nausea, hot flushes, sweating, headaches, and hypotension.

These findings are startling in that they also discovered that some medications such as monoamine oxidase inhibitors or (MAOI) used to treat depression can make patients sensitive to amines(specifically tyramine)found in cheese, fermented foods (red wine, soya products, yeast, pickled fish.

Amines Cadaverine (found in cured meat and fish, some vegetables and fruit)

Dopamine (cheese, chocolate)

Histamine (cheese, and a wide variety of sources) histamine is produced in the human body in response to allergy.

Over-ripe fruit increases amines

An addiction to chocolate , when you are hooked on this black wonder it can result in withdrawal as potent as the individual needing his or her methadone fix ,mainly because your body has become used to the dophine receptor having been filled with a steady influx of synthetic caffeine and cocoa. A drop in dopamine occurs whenever the chocolate is withdrawing the physical symptoms occur, craving, dizziness due to the drop in sugar levels as insulin dashes to balance blood sugar, headaches, adrenaline as the body prepares you for the stress of withdrawals, which in turn be responsible for the aggression you may feel due to the adrenaline rush. I have often heard chocolate addicts remark on how their addiction to chocolate calms them, even when they have a lactose allergy due to milk sugar, we have all seen the ads for the delicious bar of chocolate as a glass of milk pores into the bar. Addiction plus allergy does not stop the chocoholic from having their fix of dopamine (It is an excess of this transmitter that is deemed responsible for schizophrenia).

Not only are they addicted to this creamy sensation but their urge to stuff as much into their dainty mouth due to their allergy creates another problem, one as big as the addiction.

Obesity, this phenomenon of allergy verses addiction, obesity, plus diabetics, dopamine, all add to a body going into freefall and chronic illness.

Coffee nicotine, tea, refined carbohydrates are part and parcel of the methadone lifestyle,

All of these are addictions leading to the wrong assumption that some people have addictive personality; this then must apply to most of the population as almost everyone has an addiction to certain foods. Most also have allergies that go undetected especially addiction to coffee,tea,chololate, crisps, sweets, certain foods, coco cola, and a host of others.

Addiction and allergy is not a term associated with large consumption of everyday foods(it is seen as hunger).this couldn't be further from the truth, facts are now emerging to show that obesity can be associated with allergies. Compulsive eating is a craving and is the physiological response to the withdrawal of foods that they can be allergic to.

The body is reacting to the food withdrawal, in the same manner that the methadone and heroin user, or the person taking prescribed drugs does when their drug of choice is removed.

Chemicals and food do cause allergies and addictions depending on our genetic makeup.

Most methadone users have the allergy addiction combination, drugs, alcohol, gluten, lactose, hay fever, conjunctivitis, eczema, asthma. Some suffer with irritable bowel which is also associated with allergy. Wheat allergy associated with a protein found in gluten can lead to ceoliac disease where the small intestine is damaged leading to malabsorption, weight loss and vitamin and mineral deficiencies, dermatitis herpetiformis(eczema) is also a form of dermatitis) ongoing medical supervision is needed with this disorder, while stopping the wheat and wheat products is a must.

This disorder is difficult to detect as it progresses slowly and the sufferer is unaware they have an allergy until they suffer with the symptoms above. Depressions, feeling tired most of the time, and loose stools, stomach cramps are part of this. If left untreated it can lead to cancer.

Lactose intolerance is another crafty allergy, and as stated above most of those taking methadone are prone to many cups of coffee or tea. This has a kick on affect because it also means a high sugar intake leading to insulin rushes and drops, putting the body under stress resulting in adrenaline release and aggression. Milk is made up of water, protein, carbohydrates, milk sugar lactose, minerals fats, and other susbances. Our body reacts to Cassin any whey which is proteins in the cow's milk.

Allergies are hives or eczema, and asthma the symptoms are diarrhoea, indigestion, vomiting, hyperactive behaviour, runny nose, ear infection, and bloating, watery eyes, black around the eyes. These occur 24 hours following infestation

Milk protein is also used in evaporated milk, cheeses, yogurt, butter, sorbets, lunch meats, many deserts, backing mixes, cereals, malts pancakes, puddings, margarines.

Calcium is important for brittle bones which is on the increase in those on methadone foods that supply these are Green vegetables, seaweed, baked beans, dried fruit but beware the latter has sugar added.

Green tea

Avoidance is the best option.

Third on the list of allergy for methadone users is eczema ,certain situations and substances causes a flare up of this disorder, heat, pollen, cold air, dust mites, certain foods. This allergy is relieved by moisturizing cream, non- alkaline soap, shampoo, antibiotics.

The old method of relieving this condition was bathing in porridge oats to stop itching or using marigolds to bath the skin.

Asthma is evident in methadone users; symptoms include wheezing, coughing, shortness of breath, sinus pain, eczema, nasal polyps. Constriction of the bronchial wall, inflammation and swelling secretion of mucus.

Triggers are chemicals (methadone is a chemical) allergens, dust, old, this is interesting in that amines used in the fermentation of wines, beer, methadone, flavouring in foods are moulds or fungi.

Bronchodilators are prescribed in the treatment of asthma, and are often a derivation of the hormone epinephrine or adrenaline. This could explain why some asthma suffers on methadone present with aggression or react angrily to simple situations. Some drugs used to treat this condition are known as (B2 –agonists) stimulate the lungs to relax, over use of these agonists drugs can bring on an asthmatic attack. Methadone comes under the brand name of agonists. It binds to the nerve cells (receptors). Anti inflammatory drugs may also be used in the treatment of asthma as the immune system is responsible for the release of antibodies (IGE) like gluten protein the immune system fails to identify the foreign body and therefore goes into attract mode.

Allergy has a partner in crime obesity, water retention is common in those with an allergy once the offending food or substance is removed from the diet the water loss is great.

Methadone users can gain weight especially around the midriff due to high sugar intake and insulin highs and lows. According to DR. Michael Rosenbaum: food sensitive's can cause the body to retain water and fat. Weight drops off whenever the allergy is detected and left out of the diet. This it backed up by DR William Philpott a clinical ecologist, he maintains that the natural brain opioid enkephalin (a group of protein molecules produces in the brain and nerve endings) when it comes in contact with allergenic food which triggers a rise in this opioid neurotransmitter that are as addictive as narcotics.

These food allergens are coffee, dairy products, wheat, eggs, and corn or rice.

Potatoes, lettuce. Research also found that 99.2 % of schizophrenic's patients are allergic to one or more substances and were diagnosed as having a drug addiction. Of these 88% were allergic to wheat, while 50% it was corn and 60% to milk.

Addiction and allergies to drugs, food,fags, chocolate, coffee, tea work in a similar manner, when first taken they cause a reaction in the body, symptoms appear ,coughing, dizziness, vomiting , nausea , these continue for a period as the body reacts to the allergic chemical or toxic substance. Over time the body becomes tolerant needing more and more, if this is not forthcoming stress occurs. The compulsion to feed the cravings is overwhelming so the allergy is hidden behind the addiction. You must eat, smoke, drink, drug, to stop withdrawals. The body adapts to the toxins leaving you dependent on the drug or food. How many have you heard heavy drinkers maintain they shall never drink again only to watch them slip into the nearest pub for a fix? What friends do you know who swear they are off chocolate, only to find they have a stack hidden behind bags of sugar in the cupboard. I myself crave fresh bread and have an allergy to the very thing I crave.

Reaction to allergies causes a decree in blood sugar leading to a craving for sweets.

Dr Rosenbaum recommendation that those suffering with allergies would benefit from including minerals such as calcium, magnesium, potassium, as they neutralize the acidity associated with allergic reaction.

It appears that vitamins and minerals could be the way forward in the treatment of both allergy and addiction. Could it be possible that those on methadone have a deficiency in the minerals that resemble our cell structure?

Those on methadone and those treating them need to examine this phenomenon only then can we make the connection between addiction and allergy saving a new generation from a prescribed opioid. Allergies and food intolerance are on the increase, ranging from ceoliac disease, Asthma, eczema, nuts, and milk. An allergy involves the immune system it is a substance which causes us to have an immunological response, protein molecules are the correct size for detection by the immune system and it is these that appear to be the culprit.

Food intolerance is not an allergy it is sensitivity to chemicals found in food. This can be intolerance to salicylates, amines, lactose, and gluten found in wheat.

Salicyates is found in food that grows in or above the ground, medicines, supplements, hygiene products or cosmetics and beauty products.

Amines are found in about 70% of the same foods as salicylates and in fish, meat, chocolate, cheese. Gluten is found in wheat, barley, oats, and rye.

Salicylates and glutamate are put in food to create flavour which was addressed in an earlier capture. Lactose is sugar found in milk and dairy products.

Both amine and salicylates are found in canned pear, sweet apples, canned mango paw, rhubarb, banana blackberries,cranberries,gooseberries,strawberries,cherry,figs,melons,redcurrant,peach,nectarine,avocado,dates, grape,olives,passion fruit, raisins, sultanas,tomatos, raspberries, cabbage, parsley, potatoes, peas, leek, beans , pickled beetroot, marrow, turnip, cauliflower, mushrooms, broccoli.

These are also high in bacon, canned fish, gravy, meat pies, luncheon meat,

Coelic disease can cause deficiency in vitamins and minerals due to malabsorption. Our body is whole, the brain and body are not disconnected. We fuel our brain by the food we digest in our gut. The body gossips to the brain which in turn talks to the endocrine system letting it know when to excrete certain hormones especially adrenaline to counteract stress, it is now known that neurotransmitters are present not only in the brain, the gut, but also the immune System, as someone who has an allergy to gluten I have experienced first hand how as a child and before having been diagnosed in my early thirties, I had the same rubbish thrown at me in school . I was lazy, lacked concentration, would never make anything of myself, and on several visits to the GP I was informed it was growing pains, a common complaint in teenage years, The fuzziness and tiredness I dealt with on a daily basis evaporated when a doctor with a good interest in my condition discovered my allergy. Until then I was unaware of the role of the immune system and how it worked. Gluten is a substance that binds to flour, and bread is made from wheat. It is now understood how most allergies have consequences for the mind. Allergic reactions occur if there is over production of antibodies in the body, the gluten found in wheat is one offender. Depression is also associated with an allergy to gluten. Serotonin is affected by an allergy to gluten; ceoliac disease is on the increase with many individuals going undiagnosed as this condition is slow at presenting itself.

Some of those on methadone are reporting with sensitivity of asthma, ceoliac disease or eczema. And a shocking number have asthma, taking the many drugs that widen the airways, while corticosteroids are prescribed to elevate eczema. Allergies are a hypersensitivity to certain substances; it is an extreme reaction to the body's immune system. Histamine appears to be the culprit this mediator can produce a rash, narrowing of the airways, or at worse a drop in blood pressure.

When someone has asthma it is the action of leukotrienes, some doctors shall give corticosteroids by mouth or in the asthmatic by way of inhaler. These are used because of their anti- inflammatory properties as they reduce swelling inside the airways. It is reported that these drugs may suppress adrenal gland function, reduce bone density, and increase the risk of glaucoma. They are also less efficient when taken with other drugs.

The methadone user who also suffers from asthma is on a cocktail of an opioid, a sympathomimetic inhaler, an anticholinergic drug depending on the severity of the condition.

Our body produces substances called leukotrienes which are chemically related to prostaglandins a group of fatty acids found in the omega twins 3 and 6. We saw how our brain needs both of these GLA and DHA for healthy functioning. Prostaglandins have a number of tasks within the body, they enhance the immune system, relax blood vessels, while helping insulin to do its task of keeping sugar levels balanced. They also protect the lining of the stomach, lower blood pressure. and warn us of inflammation in damaged tissues by way of pain. When someone has asthma they can be sure that it is leukotrienes .

Food intolerance is also on the increase and new research has shown that children who suffer from autism could have digestive problems. We have acid in our stomach which is vital for digesting the food we eat, proteins must be broken down and zinc is one of the minerals that help this process. Zinc plays a vital role in the activities of 100 enzymes in our body. It manufactures proteins and the function of insulin in the utilization of carbohydrates .healing, the function of sperm, and the immune system, it is essential for those on methadone some of which have hepatitis or H.I.V. zinc is usually deficient in individuals who have liver damage, loss of appetite, and lose of taste, rash inflamed areas around the eyeslids, mouth, or fingernails or hair loss. Zinc is found in meat, seafood, wholemeal bread, cereals, and dried pulses (beans) one of the easiest ways to consume zinc is by eating unprocessed food.

As we have mentioned depression can be attributed to certain allergies especially gluten and while a lot of research has been undertaken in dealing with specific areas and much is now emerging and written about this disease. It is usually in isolation with little connection made between addiction and allergies. To my knowledge the doctors who treat those on methadone have not looked at this side of addiction. This subject is usually dealt with from a psychological perspective .where the individual availing of this opioid is seen as dependent, weak attached, or lacking motivation. The chemical needed to fuel the neurotransmitter associated mostly with lack of motivation are adrenalin, noradrenalin which is made from dopamine. If we back track to the above capture we will notice that one of the effects of the medication given for asthma has on the adrenal gland and how it interferes with its function.

Serotonin is the mood enhancer; it also controls our eating habits, and emotion, whenever this chemical is broken down swiftly by the enzymes in the brain we get depressed, drugs such as   Prozac and Aerobat work by inhibiting serotonin reuptake maintaining that the happy neurotransmitter lingers longer at the synapse. By doing so its user has a mood elevation and feel good factor. Inhibitors such as Ednorax prohibit the reuptake of the neurotransmitter adrenalin. Antidepressants are geared to stop the reuptake Of Serotonin and Noradrenalin. The question that needs answering is why have we become a country of drug taking. By that I mean legally prescribed drugs. We need to go back to the drawing board and look at what cells need if they are to maintain Homeostasis. Let's look again at the inhibitors most commonly used, we see it time and time again, serotonin, adrenalin, associated with stress released by the adrenalin gland to counteract stressful situations known as the fight or flight syndrome. Serotonin depletion is now associated with those who eat a lot of simple carbohydrates, white bread, deep fried food, processed foods, cereal. Gone are the days of a hot bowl of the show releasing energy porridge. We are starving our neurotransmitters of the correct nutrients needed to cope in this world of continuous stress. As stated in a previous chapter, methadone takers suffer from continuous stress, the stress of trying to survive in a world of judging, lack of life skills needed to change a lifestyle built on stress. It is now common knowledge that antidepressants have side effects which are as addictive as what they are trying to come off. Methadone replaced heroin as the wonder drug the only thing it cured was handbag robbery and house breaking. The heroin addict no longer needed to rob he could collect his new opium at the GP's giving him some self respect. He also did the doctor a favour by introducing him or her to a new way of economical success. By blocking the addicts neurotransmitters with heroin's cousin the addict could go on his merry way, unaware that the side effects he or she experienced when trying to come off the drug was due to a depletion of their own natural neurotransmitter endorphin.

When we examine how serotonin is made it is easy to make the link, serotonin is a form of protein the amino acid tryptophan is made from the protein, which we can get from eating cheese, porridge, eggs, fish or chicken, this amino acid is also responsible for giving us a good night's sleep, therefore it is important to eat a balanced diet of these food rather than pop sleeping medication that does interfere with a normal sleeping pattern.

The next time you see a chicken peck the grass at the side of a motorway think tryptophan plus good mental health plus serotonin. Chicken, turkey or a slab of fresh salmon not only tastes better and is less harmful than a lifetime of addiction to Prozac or other antidepressant drugs. This also would be of benefit to methadone takers who suffer from insomnia as it helps induce sleep. A good method of ensuring you are getting your quota of tryptophan is to eat lentils, green salad, chicken, eggs, tuna and my favourite porridge.

A simple banana will help raise this much needed brain chemical as it results in a release of insulin that in time helps tryptophan to reach the brain. Foods that release sugar slowly are more beneficial for those on methadone as sugar levels are balanced for longer, avoiding the dip necessary to avoid relapse. One of the most discussed topics these methadone users complain about is insomnia, tryptophan is linked to melatonin a hormone needed if we are to avoid insomnia.

Schizophrenia is a depilating disorder; the person suffering with it struggles each day to survive, nutrients are vital to maintain the mental processes of those with Schizophrenia. I have a number of methadone users who suffer from the effects of illusions

Or delusions who are labelled as anti- social. Most suffer from anxiety and depression. Nights of walking the floor due to lack of sleep leaves them with dark cycles around their eyes, this problem is compounded by the fact they cannot read or write due to bad teaching. The common theme around schizophrenia is that it is a result of a chemical imbalance. New findings suggest that those suffering from this disorder can be helped by checking homocysteine levels. The lack of essential amino acids Vitamin (3B) niacin, allergies such as gluten and a diet high in sugar intake. Methadone has high sugar content, diet is non- existent when living in a hostel or one is excluded from friends and family, does not help, exclusion from certain strands of society is another factor.

Dairy products have taken centre stage in our diet, these are ingested daily by way of the thick sandwich with its processed ham, stuffing (more wheat) and cheese into our body may be causing you to have more down days than is necessary. As bread is consumed at most lunch times, the fast food famous sandwich has seen the proper lunch fall off the nutritional radar. Dinner is now eaten between six and seven o'clock replacing the old lunch of meat and vegetables at one o'clock. Meat which was one source of protein is replaced with more refined crabs as new fangled foreign meals replace a balanced diet of vegetables, fruit, a small helping of meat, fish or chicken.

Add to that a decline in certain minerals especially zinc needed for breaking down food in the stomach plus the famous antibiotic that doctors like to dispense, has no doubt seen a rapid decline in good gut bacteria.

Nutrition

Statistics show that individuals who survive on foods fried in hydrogenated oil, show deficiencies in the brains of the most needed essential fatty acid omega 3. As essential fatty acid is provided via the diet and cannot be synthesized by the body linolexic acid (omega 3) is essential.

Could the high numbers of methadone users presenting with depression, insomnia and stress be a result of a deficiency in this fatty acid.

Animal fats found in meat and dairy products are saturated, while vegetables are unsaturated.

Some dietary fats contain vitamins A, D, E and K. A good diet for anyone consists of protein, fats, vitamins, minerals, complex carbohydrates, water and fibre.

Proteins are the main compound for tissues and organs, growth and cells. These amino acids are essential for good health; We have eight amino acids that are replenished daily by an intake of protein found in a balanced diet.

Carbohydrates: unprocessed, unrefined fruit, some porridge (organic).

Fats provide energy for the metabolism and are a structural component of cells 30% of total intake is recommended. Olive oil, avocados are monounsaturated. Saturated fat is found in meat and dairy products. Polyunsaturated found in fish vegetable oils. Saturated fats are said to increase unwanted cholesterol in blood. Polyunsaturated and mono saturated have the opposite effect.

Cutting down on saturated fat such as hard cheese or fatty meat can lead to improved health.

Fibre: a diet low in fibre leads to constipation, a complaint associated with methadone use. The disease known as diverticulitis is associated with a low fibre diet. By eating fruit, raw vegetables, grains such as porridge which are known to be are full of fibre we can contribute to our own good health. Low fibre diets contain refined carbohydrates and are associated with obesity and heart diseases.

Water: our body is composed of 60% water and is needed to maintain metabolism (the chemical process in cells) and bowel function.

Vitamins are needed for brain, skin muscles, bones, sleep, and relaxation. We get these from a healthy balanced diet and the body stores small amounts of vitamin B and C. Vitamin B complex is known to help with depression especially those on methadone and who suffer from hepatitis or who need treatment with interferon which can cause depression.

Minerals like calcium and magnesium are needed to maintain healthy teeth and keep brittle bones at bay. A majority of methadone takers suffer from joint pain or rotten teeth. It is now known that heroin depletes calcium in the body and the high intake of sugar associated with methadone may be responsible for so many young people attending their dentist or who flash rows of gaps of missing and have to wear false teeth.

Zinc and magnesium especially the latter help with nerves and muscle contraction this mineral is also needed for nerve impulses and for many enzymes. Magnesium is found in cereals, nuts, grains, milk, fish and meat, deficiency can be due to alcohol dependency, intestinal disorder such as malaborpsion due to ceoliac disease.

Anxiety restlessness, tumours, depression, palpitations can be symptoms of deficiency in this mineral. Calcium on the other hand is abundant in the body, it is essential for cells, muscles contractions blood clotting, we get this from eggs, fish, some vegetables. The next time you watch a cat eat fish bones you can be assured it does so because that is where the best calcium resides. Control of calcium is achieved via the action of hormones. Parathyroid and calcltonin which is produced by the thyroid gland. High or low levels of calcium in the blood can disrupt cell function in muscles and nerves. Calcium channel blockers are given to individuals who suffer from angina. Vitamin B12 plays a vital role in the activity of several enzymes (substances that promote chemical reactions) this vitamin is important in the production of cells. Carbohydrates are the foods of the nervous system, the foods that contain this vitamin is liver, chicken, beef, pork, fish, eggs and dairy products. When we eat a balanced diet we get sufficient amounts of B12. Deficiency can occur when the body has an inability along with the intestine to absorb the vitamins and minerals from our diet.Malobsorption is due to an undetected allergy to gluten or wheat. Memory loss and depression may result from vitamin B deficiency.

Vitamin B12 complex is found in wheat, germ whole grain, brown rice pasta liver, kidney, fish, beans, nuts, eggs. A diet high in sugar and white flour can cause deficiency in B12 complexes as does the thyroid condition known as hyperthyroid. Those who consume high levels of alcohol or who have a dependence on drugs, then deficiency can occur as a result, though loss of appetite. Interestingly methadone users appear to suffer from depression, constipation, irritability, Insomnia, tiredness. The individual taking methadone and suffering from B12 complex deficiency can this be due to poor eating habits, or an excess of toxicity

Niacin can also play a role in enzymes; our body has thousands of these chemical structures need to function properly. Malobsorbtion is due to undetected allergy to gluten or wheat. Memory loss and depression may result from vitamin B deficiency. Enzymes need a component called a coenzyme that is found in vitamins and minerals, and we know that Enzymes play an important role in the breakdown of protein and other foods to chemicals for neurotransmitters, both in the brain and body, especially the liver.

Liver enzymes activity is increased by certain drugs such as barbiturates. Many drugs block or inhibit enzyme action. Antibiotic drugs destroy bacteria enzymes but leave human ones unaffected. Liver diseases are diagnosed due to revised enzymes. Niacin (B3) is present in cereals but is not absorbed by the body. The amino acids Tryptophan is responsible for the manufacture of serotonin and which is found in protein.

Alcohol dependency depletes Niacin as does gluten intolerance, this cause a lack of vitamins and mineral malabsorption associated with gluten intolerance. Folic acid is also important for enzymes that help to manufacture (nucleic acids) folic acid can be found in vegetables, fruit fried beans, peas, eggs, wholemeal bread. It is interesting to note that refined foods, sugar, white bread do not manufacture folic acid. Vitamin C needed to maintain healthy bones, teeth, gums, blood vessels in the production of certain neurotransmitters these chemicals are responsible for nerve impulses and the adrenaline gland hormones the immune system and its responses to infection and in the healing of wounds. Dietary sources of vitamin C come from tomatoes, green leafy vegetables, green peppers, strawberries, blackcurrants. Vitamin C is lost during cooking or keeping food warm. Smoking, traffic fumes, contraceptives can cause deficiency of this important vitamin The proportion of women on methadone are also on the contraceptive pill therefore are dealing with a double intake of chemicals that can interfere with the balance of the body.

The fruits that contain these essential vitamins like Strawberries, blackberries would be a luxury food too many of those taking methadone, the green leafy vegetables affordable to them would be at best lettuce or cabbage. Remembering that individuals who are on methadone have little or no. money due to their condition, most have children, pay high rents, must shop in the same supermarkets as ourselves, paying the hiked up prices.

This book shall refers many times to the immune system of those on methadone, mainly because the proper functioning of the immune system depends on the many vitamins or minerals it needs to complete its task of ensuring that infections or diseases are kept at bay.

We enhance this process whenever we eat a balanced diet one flush in zinc, the B vitamin family, or the list of foods and fruits that I have mentioned throughout this book.

Zinc is critical for the many processes taking place within our bodies. Enzymes break down the foods we eat into chemicals, it has many processes within the human body the most important is how it helps us when we develop the common cold. We need zinc to enhance the digestive system because its contribution is necessary for the immune defence system. The body contains enzymes which are in fact chemical compounds that help the digestive system break down the protein, complex carbohydrates, and fat needed to fuel our brain and body. These togather with the liver, pancreas, and stomach produce the essential juice that ensures an easy passage of the food we consume through the intestines. Enzymes that are devoid of zinc cannot work properly resulting in a build-up of unprocessed food particals.The body cannot recognize them so attacks what it believes to be invading bactercia. Food allergies can be a result of this process.

Farting, Crohn's disease. Irritable bowel and a blotted belly are all linked to this phenomena

If an allergy goes unrecognized it can cause untold damage, leading to inflammation or worse.

 Many of those prescribed methadone have weak immune systems and therefore are prone to the many flu and infections that lurk in our everyday lives. Perhaps doctors should investigate to establish if some of those they treat with methadone are deficient in zinc.

Allergies are ripe in the methadone community from irritable bowel, asthma, coelic disease and a host of complaints that appear to get dismissed beneath the label of druggie.

Our bodies does depends on foods rich in zinc because it is incapable of storing this precious mineral on its own. Zinc is beneficial for methadone users as it helps with a wide range of bodily tasks, from bones, kidneys, skin, and pancreas, prostate. Sore throat, multiple sclerosis (remember we have already discussed how this condition can be a result of damage to the mylthe shield) which itself is dependent on essential fatty acids.

Zinc can also help in diseases such as an under active thyroid gland, and osteoporosis. All of which are associated with daily complaints of those taking methadone.

Methadone users are no different from us, except that they pump synthetic chemicals into their bodies on a daily basis, by eating raw foods especially certain vegetables and fruit these individuals can help their gut maintain healthy bacteria. Enzymes are found in the foods we consume.

Bananas, Apples, grapes, mangoes, pinapple, soya beans, wheat, and a host of others.

These are also important as they bind to free radicals that are now known to contribute to certain cancers.

We have become a fast food nation Mr McDonalds with his red nose and clown's dress is now the best friend of many a child and adult. We consume Tran's -fat foods as easy as we sleep. The once boiled potato, cabbage and meat is almost a thing of the past as children now identify with fries, burgers, these crisp golden chips wet our taste buds setting us up for future craving of refined carbohydrates, But what are we setting our children up for? Deficiency in the body and brain, most essential fats and amino acids, vitamin B complex and minerals, disorders unknown in my day are now prevalent. Hyperactivity is the new kid on the block the one who is fed a diet of drugs as a means of keeping the child controlled. Individually it could be said is dangerous or different, so must be fed a diet of Retlin, which can only add to a brain and body fed on trans fats sugar sweets, crisps processed foods.

Perhaps those who study addiction might start by looking at the link that may exist between deficiencies in the body's fuel system, humans are fuelled by energy, and energy is got by eating certain foods, like a fire or steam engine, if it does not get a steady supply of fuel it dies out and stops.

Methadone like Heroin and alcohol, affects appetite, it deadens hunger and emotion, when an individual is fed a constant stream of drugs especially opium, then suppression of hunger leads to deficiency in the foods most needed to fuel and maintain its most important function the brain. A brain fed a cocktail of drugs cannot do the job it was meant to, that is maintaining balance of natural chemical interaction.

T- Cells are the first line of defence for the immune system, stress does nothing to enhance its prospects or strengthen it. Stress sets of a chain reaction of hormone release. It goes into adrenal overdrive with a barrage of corticosteroids flooding the body and thus suppressing the immune system, leaving it unable to defend it-self against invading bacteria. It is imperative for those prescribed daily doses of methadone to remain calm. And as I shall explore in later captures this can be done without controversy or legally perscribed drugs but with holistic methods.

Are you what you eat?'

Our body is fuelled by our daily intake of proteins carbohydrates, water, vegetables minerals and vitamins. Our nutritional value remains the same as our ancestors, the difference being that they didn't grab a trolley and fill it full of processed food dripping with chemicals.

The once sweet smelling tomato, that granny placed on the table for the evening tea, has fallen off the end of the planet, it has been replaced by the shinny scrubbed non- smelling immigrant from Europe.

Cold pressed apple juice had a natural sugar content, today it's cousin is unrecognizable as it is stuffed into a carton with a belly full of sugar,

The Sunday roast wandered aimlessly around the yard pecking at insects and bits of rubbish, unaware that its destiny was to have its head struck in a steel cage eating its weight in processed grain, its overflowing belly dragging the ground, as this suffering conveyer bird, was oven ready in pronto time, so its owner could relish in his profit adding another foreign holiday to his list of "do's"

The headache, anxiety, sore toe, were treated with respect, they were taken for a walk in the fresh air.

The human metabolism, endocrine system, neurotransmitters, liver, panaceas, were not informed about the twenty century processing machine, or pharmacology breakthroughs in how synthetic drugs could bind to receptors like a tight dress on Kate Moss

It had to learn the hard way from experience, accept what was ingested into its gut and hope for the best. The problem is the body was unable to cope with the numerous amounts of both processed foods, prescribed medication, pollutes, and a flotilla of hidden chemicals that it must deal with on a daily basis. Heroin was something you took for the trauma of war, to get you through the shock of killing a fellow human.

That is until the war lords of Afghanistan saw the humble poppy as a commercial viable commodity, discovering that they could make a few bucks on the misery of dole depended Europeans.

So the flooding of these countries began, with more and more youth hell bent on hiding from their problems with the preverbal high, strung out on brown glue.

The gentle poppy suddenly thrust into the limelight" as the in thing", the ultimate buss, a friend coming all the way from the East, to unleash devastation on its user

The body is a complex machine; it must be fed a daily intake of certain foods to maintain a healthy balance, foods that are converted into the chemicals which give us energy to function. A depletion or deficiency in these body building blocks can knock it side-way leaving it volatile and open to the many bacteria waiting to disturbed its equilibrium.

In order to maintain a healthily mind we must feed it what shall keep everything balanced. If we are intent on throwing scraps of junk into our body on a daily basis with little respect for the consequences then we must take responsible for the choices we make in regard to its welfare.

As children we were lined up each Saturday and presented with seeny pod (to clear us out),

A glass of thick butter milk was drunk to put a lining on our stomach, cabbage water to kill thread worms and to make iron, fresh blackberries and strawberries to ensure healthy eyes.

The seeny pod was a killer; the butter milk followed a close second.

What I didn't know then but know now was that MA had a good insight into what was good to maintain healthy bacteria in the gut. Her green pleading eyes standing over us like a corporal making sure every last drop of the horrible smelly milk slipped down our throats, as she ensured we got our quota of lactobacillus and bifodobacteria. Mother was ahead of her time, she could have patented buttermilk making us all a fortune.

Visit any supermarket today and you shall see shelves lined with rows of this commodity which is revered by some in the medical profession as the new James Bond of cholesterol.

Bacteria are a duel whammy we need it but it can also harm us. There goes that word again balance. learning to balance our diet is an important step in looking after our own health.(think about that doctors would become redundant, no more having to pay 70euro for them to inform us we are not well.

Much research has concluded that fermented milk does improve our health. This revelation has sent probiotics profits scoring. So much has been attributed to this milky substance that it has been introduced into animal feed to enhance growth. (Remember antibiotics)

This matrix of the sour milk family is found in cottage cheese, yoghurt.bread made from rye or wheat, soya, tofu, (found in health shops) and sauerkraut which is eaten mostly in Germany and Poland, but can be found in certain shops.

These come with a hefty C...V. from lowering cholesterol, boosting the immune system, reducing certain forms of cancer, relieving irritable bowel, and helping in the production of vitamins.While helping with ingestion. Constipation, or prolonger stress.

We know that methadone uses who suffer with a combination of these symptom have a range of these conditions. We know that for our body to maintain homeostasis it must be fed a proper diet.

Continuous drinking of methadone was not on the nutritional agenda for a homeostatic balance. We know that whenever someone suffering from cancer is given a morphine pump they can lose their appetite

I am often told that they don't feel hungry due to the drug.

Good bacteria is essential if we are to maintain good health which can be found in a range of fresh fruit and vegetables and are a better source to prepare your body to fight infections, high cholesterol,marshling your hormones, those chemical substances needed not only for metabolism, stress, anxiety, but the interaction between brain .and body

By ensuring you eat only fresh food, or better still grow your own in tubs on the patio, that way you know they are devoid of the chemicals that can play havoc with an already ready weak immune system.

By feeding your gut good bacteria you will contribute to their expansion and growth, which in turn destroys bad bacteria in the gut.

Our body needs protein but it doesn't need this in the form of an over-load of meat on a daily basis, protein can also be found in certain nuts, beans and vegetables.

When your mother reminded you to drink your buttermilk and give your belly a rest, she was passing on good advice not only for your gut but your over-all health.

Deep-fried

Oils that we fry our chips in can also have an effect on the functioning of the liver. These vegetable oils are heated at high temperatures and are used in processed foods, junk foods, like buggers, chicken nuggets, these come under the fancy name as Trans fats. They interfere with the detoxification process of the liver causing deposits of fat to lodge in the liver, bile becomes blocked and its efficiency is derailed.

The good old tablet also has a negative influence on the over tired liver causing damage

These are drugs to lower cholesterol

Anti- inflammatory drugs.

Birth control drugs

Hormones

If you are on these for long periods you should request a liver test.

One way of helping the liver to eliminate toxins is to drink watered down cranberry juice this is also good for the kidneys, of course what better way to give your liver a helping hand than to drink water instead of coffee or soft drinks. We encounter it all around us, people stuffing their mouths with foods deep fried.

The cod and chips pit stop at weekends is part and parcel of our lives. People queuing at the chipper to indulge in the deep fried fantasy.

What then is this pleasurable experience doing for our brains or body? It is causing a catalogue of health problems.

The casting vote for deep-fried food does over rule common sense when it comes to proper eating habits.

There is no doubt that the body needs fat, but these are not found in convenience foods resting on supermarket shelves.

Constrain is not a word associated with someone who needs instant gratification.

The gratification for a serotonin rush can be fulfilled by stuffing ones face on buggers, chips fast food. It is difficult to discontinue these unhealthy eating habits, the disadvantage is a sudden drop in the neurotransmitter serotonin that is needed to elevate mood.

One must be much disciplined to stop this marry go- round the effort can be as difficult as the methadone user trying to come down on his or her green diesel.

Convenience foods do not only have added salt and sugar (usually dresses up as a fancy word on the packaging) but they do have hidden dangers for health. Some oils are heated at high temperance's. This process of hydrogenation which is of no nutritional value to your body potatoes are fried in oil, heat oxidises when subjected to high temperance's this destroys antioxidants. If we become deficient in these antioxidants we are streaming headlong into health deficient waters.

We are all dependant on the air we breathe, this oxygen works on the cellule body, and its role is the releasing of energy to survive

Like a slow worm it is harmless until it is hampered with. We know for instance that you never light a match around oxygen, otherwise it may combust. Now think chipper, the fry, sunny day barbecuing and you are staring at a face as old as the sugar-loaf mountain, health as bad or worse as your dear auld granny . And perhaps a liver that looks as if you slugged booze down your throat all your life. The fancy term that is doing the rounds today is free radicals, we are not talking a group of visionaries, we are talking health hazards, those caused by continuously violating your health by consuming fried foods.

It is implausible to comprehend the daily drilling that some methadone users give their body's in their quest for the good old fry-up in oils that oxidise and cause free radicals, like an incendiary device waiting to happen, not only the methadone user, but for all who refuse to explore this menace

If we subject ourselves to years of antioxidant deficiency we are heading into an avalanche of not only mental illness but diabetes, cancer, Alzheimer's disease, eye degernation.and inflammation.(The methadone users list toper)... Disarming free radicals is a daunting task as it involves an overall change in dietary habits. But help is at hand in the form of a proper balanced eating regime, one containing antioxidant, in the form of red tomatoes, berries, grapes, broccoli, some herbs especially turmeric that used in many Indian curries.

Prunes have a double whammy as they work as fibre which is great for the methadone taker. Spinach a lovely vegetable and it is so easy to cook, the best way is to sweat this dark green vegetable in a little butter with some herbs.

The good old solid curly kale that Dublin is famous for and known in most countries around the world is another wonder food.

Plums another resourceful fruit, lushes and great in a smoothie.

Avocados, all kinds of berries, alfalfa sprouts, some of which can be grown in your own kitchen as easy as walking the dog.

The next times you address your face in the mirror ask yourself an honest question...
"Is the colour of you shin, the aging of your face and the dullness of your eyes down to free radicals due to eating food that could be killing you?

Chemical Dance (stress)

Stress, depression, insomnia are all part of methadone use. We all encounter stressful situations and when we do the body prepares itself for the threat by a quick hormone release of adrenaline and energy release to the liver. Blood pressure, sweating, heart rate. The spleen releases more blood cells and bone marrow is involved in fighting stress. The hypothalamus is the stress centre of the brain. Norepinephine works on the pituitary gland releasing extra sugar from the liver. It also releases AETH the stress hormone which stimulates the adrenaline gland which releases cortisol that regulates the release of glucose and minerals.

Stress depletes our body's vitamins and minerals leaving us prone to illness. It can also impair the immune system in its ability to fight infection. Stress is now linked to conditions such as heart disease. People who work in certain jobs such as an assembly line, family demands, especially among methadone users can adversely affect health, as some of those on methadone usually live in chronically stressful settings, they do not have adequate financial resources for daily living, *can* be poorly educated, *so* have little or no chance of finding a job. They also suffer the double whammy of social exclusion or snobbery about where they reside. Most come from areas riddled with drugs therefore can be stigmatised as being the same.

The immune system is affected by stress it contains specialized cells called lymphocytes that protect the body from disease causing microorganisms. Stress it is now known can interfere with the immune system's ability to defend the body. We are more likely to suffer from a cold when we are stressed. Allergies, cigarettes and alcohol, bad diet also influence and weaker the immune system.

A study carried out by (Jemmott 1985) found that stressful events such as death, divorce, exams, and job pressures could evaluate the immuncopetence lowering antibodies in the blood that helps defend against infections.

Research carried out by (Kiecolt and Glaser 1985) showed that we can reduce stress and help to avert immunological changes by doing relaxation, meditation. These findings could help explain why Reiki, Meditation, Acupuncture appear to help those on methadone to cope better with emotional problems that cause stress.

Lack of control appears to be linked to stress as we witness in people who believe they are not in control of their lives or situation. Most of those who abuse drugs think they have no control over their condition they believe they are helpless to do something about their lives; drugs give them the illusion of control. The same applies around methadone the individual who wants to come down on the amount of vie they consume each day; can change their mind on being told by their doctor that they are not yet ready. Our immune system is like a large power house, with a complex working system to defend the body. It does not work independently but like the brain works in harmony with other areas of the body. Stress affects our nervous system, which in turn affects hormones which are released from the adrenaline gland. The immune system is the body's first line of defence and goes into attack mode at anything it deems alien. It is now believed that lymphocytes have receptors like neurotransmitters, so our immune system cells like brain cells can receive messages from our nervous system to react. This makes sense when we consider that stress, depression, anxiety which is emotional can deplete levels of neurotransmitters.

Most stressful situations that those on methadone deal with centre around emotional states
Such as family, extended family,
Housing,
Separation or divorce
Children, school, trouble with the law
Financial, not enough money to pay bills
Education lack of
Sexual difficulties, methadone can and does cause low libido in both sexes
Death
Homelessness
Trouble with in-laws
Health
Or plain survival

Whenever we are stressed we set in motion a chemical dance, the body releases adrenal to prepare us for the fearful event, either to confront it or to run like hell and avoid it.

This flight of fight phenomena sends our body into chemical overdrive as it flushes hormones into the blood stream. Both adrenal and cortisol which change the heart-rate, blood pressure, metabolism. Once the stressful situation abates adrenal slowly returns to normal leaving its running mate cortisol lingering much longer.

Raised cortisol sends a negative message back to the body and brain that it is about to experience A famine encouraging the liver to release glucose , the pancreas to release insulin, reciprocates by redoubling its affords to restore fat leading to binging on foods that are sweet and give instant gratification, such as chocolate, coffee, chips.

Stress is a lamb in wolves clothing, its double take in preparing the body for trouble and strive by releasing adrenal and cortisol into the blood stream, the result is an appetite as ravenous as a starved monk, and weight gain in places that you would rather it avoided, your midriff.

Stress is a negative emotion it can contribute to those taking methadone to relapse to a lifestyle or behaviour that can destroy them, they do so because of their inability to cope with the many challenges life throws at them. Chronic stress is a part and parcel of methadone use.

Some have spent most of their childhoods enduring stressful home life situations such as alcohol abuse, domestic violence, poverty or emotional neglect. Stress may have been a part of their lives. They have become conditioned to helplessness, hopelessness; the least stressful response sets them off. The news of a death of a neighbour may cause anxiety as they associate this with a parent. News of a Child's illness can send shock waves of mixed emotions especially if the individual is separated from his or her own children setting a string of emotional events like guilt, shame, blame. As most may be divorced or at worse have neglected their children thought years of drugging.

(AJnomson 1978) referred to this as learned helplessness. The negative event is internalized by blaming themselves which in turn sets off a chain reaction of anxiety, that can lead to other negative behaviour. The father who believes he will never get employment because he has little or no education may find other means of acquiring the material things for his family. This gives him a feeling of being in control whatever the circumstances and it also stops the anxiety of feeling helpless. Perhaps the reason many of those on methadone who attend a program and start to build self esteem. By doing something about their predicament they have taken back control and have some hope for their future.

Knowledge about neurotransmitters and the effect of drugs, diet, education, computers, relaxation, stress associated with anxiety is side lined for the few hours that they can concentrate on self. They have support, someone who listens and unlike society does not judge.

Until we as a society learn to deal with stressful situations in a more natural way, other than stuffing antidepressants into our mouths, and when doctors take a more open ended view of understanding alternative ways of looking at stress ,depression, anxiety, by way of diet, neurotransmitters, hormones, we shall see a country unable to deal with emotion and stress.

There are a few far-sighted doctors out there, but not enough to counteract the many who give a quick fix to another-wise fixable problem

Foul Mood:

Depression is a response to life's stresses. It can be caused by emotion, disappointment, a lack of motivation, sadness, feelings of rejection, it can be a host of symptoms or the person may find themselves crying for no reason. Some who are depressed over a period of time may try to take their own life. Suicide is on the rise especially amongst these who have to struggle each day with a drugs problem. They lose interest, motivation comes to a grinding halt, they can't see their way past a negative thought and see themselves as a piece of shit, a failure, low- self esteem grabs their hand as they sink deeper into depression. One of the first things that occur is loss of appetite, insomnia, loss of energy, fatigue.

Less of appetite, insomnia, energy loss and fatigue are interesting in that these do not only happen to depressed people, similar symptoms occur to individuals who do not eat a proper nutritional diet. Any individual who does not get the correct amount of vitamins or minerals, essential fatty acids, or amino acids is not only starving their physical body but the brain and body because both need nutrition's to survive. To fight infection, to make chemicals that send messages to our nerves, hormones, muscles. Serotonin is the neurotransmitters associated with depression; a deficiency in this neurotransmitter is believed to cause depression. Serotonin is a substance found in many tissues especially blood platelets, the lining of the digestive tract, and the brain. In the brain it works as a neurotransmitter, a chemical involved in nerve impulses between nerve cells. In the digestive tract it inhibits gastric secretion stimulating smooth muscles in the intestinal wall, it also controls consciousness and mood. Serotonin neurotransmitters are disrupted by drugs like LS.D and other drugs.

In order to give our brain amino acids of which are a group of chemical compounds found in protein? We have 20 amino acids in our body that make up protein, twelve of which is made by the body. The remaining eight known as essential amino acids can only be obtained from our diet. Therefore if we are feeding our faces on refined carbohydrates, like the thick fresh batch loaf stuffed with hard cheese, rashers and sausages, fried egg, black pudding, wolfing down chocolate bars, large mugs of tea or coffee, with three to four spoonfuls of sugar, followed by the fag, tap yourself on the back you have just set yourself up for free fall and a mood downer by a drop in serotonin levels. Neurotransmitters need to be fed not on foods that deplete your energy levels following the initial high of sugar and refined carbohydrates. To keep our mood balanced we need to eat foods rich in complex carbohydrates, such as fruit, protein found in vegetables, beans, lentils and peas. Perhaps that's the secret of Victoria Beckhams cloth's horse figure she is reported to eat peas (frozen). Nuts and seeds can replace the chocolate biscuits, brown rice mixed with rested vegetables with a little olive oil instead of chips, chicken and vegetable that has not had a life cooped up in a dirty cage, or vegatables that had the life cooked out of them. The person suffering from depression could be contributing to their own condition that is if the condition is not caused by an inherited gene. Whenever we eat a balanced diet of the foods needed to feed our brains, body or nervous system we contribute to our own mental health. One of the other symptoms associated with depression is lack of motivation. Again, we need to eat the correct foods for the release of neurotransmitter dopamine, adrenaline, noradrenalin, GABA, acetylcholine. Acetylcholine is the neurotransmitter found at synapse throughout the nervous system we need it for maintain good memory. Dopamine Is a neurotransmitter released from nerve endings. A deficiency in dopamine is known to be the cause of Parkinson's disease. Dopamine is used to shock the heart back into action following heart failure.

GABA: inhibitory transmitter in the nervous system, we need it to control muscle movement. Drugs used to treat anxiety can contain some properties that are related to a facilitation of GAB inhibitory activity. Mood- altering drugs such as LSD and chlorpromazine can cause an excess of deficiency in neurotransmitters. Drugs used to treat schizophrenia block the neurotransmitter dopamine stopping messages getting through. Serotonin is a neurotransmitter known as (5-HT) synthesized in neurons in the central nervous system. (ENS) and cells in the gastrointestinal tract. It plays an important role in anger, aggression, and body temperature. Moods, sleep, appetite, sex and metabolism. It is found in mushrooms, fruits, vegetables. It has broad activities in the brain, serotonin receptors and the transporter which help reuptake into presynapes can have a role in neurological diseases. Serotonin is released from (swellings) and not from synaptic terminals which other transmitters do. It diffuses over a wide gap and activates receptors on the dendrites the thin like branches cells bodies and presynapic terminals to adjacent neurons (cells). Serotonin receptors are located on the cell membrane of nerve cells we get serotonin from an amino acid tryptophan.

Tryptophan is the precursor to serotonin which is necessary for transmitting nerve impulses in the brain including sleep and calmness. Tryptophan is needed to make serotonin, any deficiency will lead to depression, insomnia and as tryptophan converts to niacin (B3) and vitamin (B6) it is important if we are to keep both depression and lack of sleep at bay we need dietary sources of food rich in these amino acids.

These are brown rice,

Cottage cheese,

Peanuts,

Meat,

Turkey.

It is essential for biochemical balance in the brain especially for these methadone takers who suffer sleep deprivation, anxiety and depression due to low serotonin levels. Methadone is a chemical addiction it is a sister of heroin and is known to be more addictive, the individual coming off this drug needs to do so under the supervision of a doctor as it has similar withdrawal symptoms, sweating, muscle cramps, vomiting, and severe pain. Cocaine which is a chemical addiction causes a deficiency of dopamine also causing serotonin neurotransmitter imbalance.

Some clinics dealing with addiction administer tryptophan and tyrosine to help counteract neurotransmitter imbalance. Sleep deprivation is a serious concern for most methadone user's deficiency in tryptophan is responsible. While tryptophan can be taken in supplement I would recommend that anyone on methadone should consult their doctor for advice before doing so. Complex carbohydrates and a vitamin B6 is a better option as both are needed to make serotonin. A diet high in sugar, refined carbohydrates or sweets, fries, Trans fats shall keep you awake doing nothing to enhance sleep. Serotonin is essential for neurotransmitter communicating nerve cells talk to each other by chemical interaction without inadequate levels of serotonin we would suffer from depression, sleep disorder and addictions.

The best way to get the amino acid tryptophan is to ensure you eat food high in carbohydrates when we do so we release insulin which cleans other amino acids in the blood allowing tryptophan free reign to do the job it was intended to do.

(Richard and Judith wentruam) researchers from Massachusetts have shown that meals high in carbohydrates can help this amino acid enter the brain

(Dr Albert Stunkard) professor of psychiatry at the University of Pennsylvania believes that when we sneak into the kitchen at night to gorge ourselves on certain foods we are trying to boost serotonin levels. Women who diet suffer a drop in serotonin levels. As a majority of women on methadone gain weight and go on a diet they need to be careful they don't suffer a drop in serotonin. Perhaps this could be the reason why some resort to alcohol to compensate for low serotonin.

Research carried out at Oxford University on 15 men and women found that three weeks on a low calorie diet reduced tryptophan levels especially in the 15 women in comparison to the15 men. Women going through the menopause can suffer symptoms of depression, low mood; sleeplessness due to reduced oestrogen levels which is needed to increase serotonin receptors in the brain, a reduction has the opposite effect.

The majority of those on methadone smoke, some quite heavily. An explanation could below serotonin levels as nicotine increases serotonin levels, when a smoker tries to quite they can have a change in mood. It is not uncommon to see someone intent on quitting a smoking habit gain weight. They shall have increased appetite due to the withdrawal of nicotine therefore drop in serotonin levels. As we saw earlier aggression, mood, depression, sleep deprivation all deplete serotonin this could be one reason why most methadone users have difficulty in quitting their smoking habit. If their diet is deficient in vitamins, minerals, amino acids and essential fats, nicotine is ensuring a rise in serotonin allowing then to remain calm, sleep and keep moods even. Tryptophan is the amino acid that manufactures serotonin which is responsible for pain tolerance associated with arthritis and osteoporosis. It also helps control appetite so eating nutrition essential foods rich in tryptophan is important for methadone takers as it helps them control sugar blood levels and adrenaline depletion. Balanced sugar levels means less symptoms associated with methadone use, Poor concentration, sweating, insomnia, fatigue, thirst and depression. As tryptophan and serotonin go hand in glove and helps control the appetite, by stopping foods such as sugar, refined carbohydrates, buns, biscuits, sweets and cakes the person on methadone can do much to bring about a change in mood. By taking control of their diet and smoking they can take control of their methadone intake.

Glaser who wrote Choice Theory maintained that depression could be used as a means of control. The depressed person does not have to take responsible, can receive sympathy from family, friends, doctors, and employer, in today's society depression can get the individual a life time

Of social welfare. Methadone has the same effect ,most of those on this addictive drug, can receive disability benefit ,rent allowances, free school books, money for furniture on moving into a new home .Methadone is the companion of depression, and depression is a word that sends many doctors grabbing their pads scribbling a prescription for antidepressants.

By refusing to examine factors such as methadone mixed with alcohol which depletes its potency by almost fifty percent and is highly dangerous, a fact overlooked by many of those on methadone. Duel drugging is also prevalent in those that use methadone; a factor associated with depression constant prescribing of antidepressants without counselling can trap the individual into a lifetime of helplessness.

Holding them hostage to years of addiction and prescribed drugs.

I Can't Sleep:

As seen from previous chapters insomnia can be due to low serotonin levels. As the amino acid tryptophan is a precursor of serotonin and an imbalance can be genetic or bad eating habits especially one high in refined carbohydrates. Protein in the food we eat is made up of strands of amino acids, these form neurotransmitters (chemicals) that our body needs to send messages throughout the body. Tryptophan is only one of these and manufactures serotonin. Whenever we have low levels of these neurotransmitters we seek a quick fix by eating refined carbohydrates, smoking, or taking drugs especially cocaine. Overweight individuals are compelled to eat more due to low serotonin levels as refined carbohydrates help to raise serotonin temporarily.

Methadone individuals suffer from a range of symptoms that indicate they could be deficient in the neurotransmitter serotonin. Depression, insomnia, aggression, mood changes, lack of energy, High sugar intake, smoking, coffee and tea drinking. Sleep deprivation is a serious complaint driving most people to their limits. Those on methadone usually receive sleeping pills adding to a body topped up on opium. I have yet to meet one of these individuals who have had a serotonin count or dietary information that could help fix the problem of insomnia in a more natural way. What we eat affects our sleep as some food revives our brain while others help to calm us. Tryptophan is now connected to a good night's sleep. This amino acid makes serotonin which slows down nerve traffic allowing our brain to relax. Foods which keep us awake stimulating neurotransmitters that perk the brain into action should be avoided, those on methadone need to be made aware of foods that produce tryptophan because it is important in the manufacture of the sleep inducing substance serotonin and melatonin. It is the raw material that the brain needs to build the neurotransmitters needed to help us relax.

Eating foods containing this amino acid can help us to avoid sleepless nights. In order for those on methadone or the individual suffering from insomnia to get good nights kip they could try eating a bowl of wholegrain cereal with milk, or a glass of milk oatmeal and raisins, cookies, wholemeal bread with peanut butter. Comfort food such as apple pie and ice cream is the perfect snack about one hour before settling down for the night. Dairy products like cottage cheese, milk, seafood, whole grains, brown rice, eggs, sunflower seeds, hazelnuts, beans, chicken or turkey for dinner all of these foods contain the amino acids that is needed to make serotonin and melatonin.

High protein and carbohydrates should be eaten at lunch and breakfast. Dinner should consist of a meal high in complex carbohydrates and only a small amount of protein like scrambled eggs and cheese, meat with vegetables, tuna and salad sprinkled with sesame seeds, chicken with red peppers and garlic.

Those on methadone's like those individuals who suffer from insomnia and therefore have difficulty getting to sleep can be the can be contributing to their condition due to their eating habits. A change in their diet could enhance and improved their overall health, dispel anxiety and depression and have the added bonus of helping them to prepare to come off methadone. I do state here the latter should only be undertaken under the correct supervision of their doctor.

By watching what we eat and gathering as much information as possible about what chemicals are used in the processing of shelf life foods those on methadone can help build better sleeping patterns.

A Bit of Crack:

Consuming alcohol is acceptable in many western societies. To abstain from drink is to be different, dull, boring, a spoil sport. Governments receive large revenue returns from taxing alcohol.

From being born to dying is celebrated by a drinking session. This potentially dangerous drug is responsible for halving the strength of methadone, but most methadone users don't appear to make the connection. Indulging in drink binges at weekends, leaving them self open to withdrawals or mood changes totally ignoring or suffering the after- effects of vitamin and mineral deficiency following high consumption of alcohol which is it-self a depressant by depressing the central nervous system in the same manner as methadone. And like morphine, or tranquilisers alcohol is also responsible for symptoms similar to the above as it can also cause dependency, craving and withdrawal symptoms. Methadone is opium like drug. An opium derivative such as morphine, codeine, and methadone are synthetic. Studies indicate that there is the possibility of a relationship between certain chemical deficiencies and the prosperity for addiction to depressants. Heroin is established as causing an endorphin deficiency as the receptors become dependent on the external depressants. Alcohol is not only consumed, it is perfumes, paints and body sprays and antiseptics. Alcohol production occurs by way of the fermentation process that occurs when sugar reacts with yeast, fruit grains and vegetables are used in this process. It raises lipoproteins when taken in moderation especially wine. Barley and malt grains are fermented to make beer, while grapes are fermented to make wine. Like heroin and tranquilisers alcohol is a mind altering chemical it acts as a stimulant as it releases dopamine because alcohol is absorbed through the small intestine foods slow this process down. Most alcohol drinkers become hungry especially for fried food or trans-fats it is these foods that slow down absorption in the body it affects the inhibitors in the brain and becomes acetaldehyde. Heavy drinkers can suffer liver damage, acetaldehyde mixes with the neurotransmitters and by causing a chemical that attaches to receptors they get a similar effect as morphine leaving the heavy drinker with an addiction to this drug alcohol something similar to the heroin addict or methadone user.

As alcohol is made from grain, fruits, vegetables, it makes calories perhaps this explains why most heavy drinkers pile on weight. Research undertaken by (Blur 1990) concluded that alcoholism appears to be related to an abnormality of the dopamine receptor gene. (Gully 1995) made the connection between serotonin and drinking alcohol decreases the white blood cells, damages the liver which is needed to fight disease, depletes the body of vitamins and minerals, causes brain damage when taken with sedatives or barbiturates it can result in death. Not to mention driving, like heroin it produces withdrawal symptoms, shakes, diathermia, nausea, anxiety, panic attacks, confusion and long term use can result memory impairment due to cell destruction when nutrition becomes depleted

Don't fry my brain:

As stated in the previous chapter our body needs vitamins and minerals which we get from balanced diet of meat, fish, vegetables, fruit, fibre, nuts, seeds, omega 3 and 6. If we continue to feed children a diet high in sugary foods and processed foods a diet lacking in vegetables or fruit can we be surprised if as teenagers they show symptoms of depression, drug addiction, present with food allergies associated with high intakes of wheat and gluten which can cause   not only a lack of concentration but are unable to remember spelling, maths or reading. We now have a growing number of those in the medical profession who have accepted that while we do need some drugs to combat illness we could go a long way to dispel the many self inflicted disorders that are associated with a diet lacking proper nutrition. Children's brains are the same as ours, to ensure they have healthy neurotransmitters and receptor sites they must receive proper amino acids. The brain is more than half fat. Fried food and pollution contribute to getting oxidants into our body and which do nothing to counteract the damage. Essential fats are needed because they manufacture certain components that protect the brain while Tran's fats which are sold in fast food outlets contribute to stifle and slow down the brain. The deep fat fryer resting in the kitchen is the cupid of frying not only food but your child's brain. The fag you puff longingly exhaling the smoke into your child's face or sending a plum of oxidants into the atmosphere helps you move a step further to ensuring that your children shall suffer from zinc depletion.

As your treasured child grows the zinc deficiency experienced by your child though transfats, smoking, refined carbohydrates, can deplete serotonin levels, causing depression, insominia. And when the teacher informs you that your child lacks motivation, or is not achieving at school, or indulges in destructive behaviour, look closer at the child's eating habits. When we feed our Children an inappropriate diet when young, we are setting a pattern for life. If their diet consists of foods that are processed, sugar, fries, deep fried then you are not giving them the nutrition needed for concentration, remembering, staying alert or good memory. Research under- taken at James hospital Ireland, found that smoking was responsible for psychotic symptoms in the individuals who suffered from bipolar disorder. In working with manic depressive individuals it was interesting to note that most not only smoked but indulged in countless cups of coffee and tea, many had allergies and eat a diet high in refined or fatty foods. When put on omega 3 and a B12 complex they remained stable and could think clearly holding down a job for longer. Another interesting factor was that when they changed their eating habits they had fewer breaks in mental functioning.

Zinc is a mineral a deficiency is said to results in mental health problems such as anxiety ADHD delinquency, depression and schizophrenia. Research undertaken with children, suggested those children who received supplements of zinc preformed better at tasks on memory and attention. Zinc is found in foods such as fresh fruit, vegetables, nuts, lentils, brown rice. By cutting down on refined carbohydrates, sugary foods, ice cream, sweets, crisps, fizzy high powered drinks, biscuits and cakes you are protecting your child from deficiencies in many of the most important vitamins and minerals needed to ensure good memory, attention, concentration, hyperactivity, aggression and more importantly allowing your child to maintain a balanced body and mind so they are less likely to turn to drugs either illegal or prescribed.

Light Fantastic

The human body is a pulsing dynamic field of energy. In medical terminology this is known as the bio magnetic energy field or "Aura". Cameras can pick up our energy field showing different colours of pulsing, light moving around us. Everyone's aura is different and changes constantly depending on our moods, thoughts, environment and health. Individuals who abuse drugs are reported to have a grey aura which is slow moving. Like people who are suffering from illness their aura is depleted or damaged.

Negative thoughts or behaviour. Chemicals, especially those pollutants that are expelled into the atmosphere like pesticides or herbicides, bad diet, addictive substances and stress all contribute to aura blockages. In order to understand how energy is produced we shall examine how it is formed within our body and the important role the liver play in converting food into energy so we can survive.

The brain according to Dr. Karl Pullman is essentially holographic. Its structure sight, hearing, taste, smell distributes the information throughout the whole body. The brain employs a holographic domain that transcends time and space.

Reiki is outside linear time and space. It is not understood by medicine for this reason. Acupuncture suffered the same fate until it was firmly accepted and it is now used as an anaesthetist by some far sighted doctors.

Meditation also transcends linear time. The individual transcends linear thoughts. Scientific theory is just that a hypothesis put forward by an individual. It remains in place until some other scientific brain comes up with a better experiment or idea that builds or disproves that theory. (J.S. Bell 1964) did just that to Einstein's Relativity Theory that particles cannot travel faster than the speed of light. Bell's theory disproved Einstein's in that he proved that effects are faster than the speed of light. To date it could be suggested that these wise man have brought us closer to understanding energy fields.

The universe is a whole, like the body it is a web of interacting probabilities. We are connected to the universe, not inseparable from it. Healers can tap into this energy in their work; they become channels of energy to allow healing from the powers that be. They open themselves up to love, coming to the realisation that they are like the particles of the universe. Working with energy fields higher frequencies. Our higher bodies are connected to the universe. Christ was depicted in paintings with a glowing light around his head. Was this his extended consciousness with his father (God)? Christ healed by his hands, Mohammad and Moses healed by their hands they opened their hearts to love, and forgiveness, they became channels for God's love and healing energy.

Parma or Universal Energy, this breath of light moves through every form of life, plants, animals, humans all have cells that need light, sunshine and water to grow and develop.(Dr. William Kilmer 1911) Discussed how a coloured light mist existed around the body. This human energy field consisted of a dark layer closest to the body, with a second and third layer streaming from the body whenever diseases showed up as patches or irregularities within the aura. Alcohol, drugs, negative thinking are all said to deplete the energy field. Research carried out by Dr. Kilmer suggests that liver infection, tumours, epilepsy or psychological distress can be observed by colour change in the aura. There is natural field of energy that surrounds the ethnic body displays a natural rhythm when in a healthy state. If however, we have surgery or illness the energy levels are changed. Organs adjacent to that which has been removed is altered.

The body according to many studies can be viewed as a concept of energy. The universal energy field, pulsing in a synchronised rhythm. This rhythm of energy is blocked by physical psychological or mental factors. Drugs are like a dark cloud that encircles the body blocking the energy from swirling in its natural rhythm, resembling the earth's atmosphere blocked from the sun's rays.

If I were to hold a crystal a few yards from a plant I would feel the plant's energy. Our aura is connected to our chakras. The first chakra is associated with the first aura. This had to do with feeling pain or pleasure as it is located near the sexual organs. Our autonomic system is also aligned with this chakra. This controls the smooth muscles which include the heart, blood vessels, and lining of the stomach. Digestion and circulation are regulated by this system even as we sleep. It has two divisions, whenever we become emotionally excited this system speeds up the heart, and constricts the digestive organs.

The para-sympathetic division is responsible for bowel dischargment in times of fear both systems interact in complex ways. The association between the aura and second chakra is to do with emotions, our feelings of hurt, anger, frustration, self-pity, victimhood. Mental life is connected to the third or solar plexus which is yellow in colour when we have a healthy or positive attitude.

The fourth chakra is affiliated with the fourth layer of the aura. This is the heart where all conditional love flows. Love for the self, family, humanity all around us. Society and family sometimes have a blocked chakra as they give conditional love. "I love you because you do as I want". This level of the aura and chakra is usually blocked in individuals who abuse substances due to years of conditional love, that in turn lead to low self-esteem, self-hatred, guilt, anger, shame, distrust.

The fifth level of the aura is connected to throat, speech, listening and accepting responsibility for actions. By unblocking it the healer opens the person to speaking out about the past and present hurts. Individuals who are bullied have a closed fifth chakra. Constant put down negative comments can be attributed to fear of speaking your truth.

The sixth level is connected with love from a higher source. It is unconditional, the type associated with non-judgemental attitude. Counsellors display this in their work. They listen refusing to pass judgement. They allow the individual to develop and grow into their full potential without fear, shame guilt. Choice is seen as important. Limitations do not exist in the session. Control, hurt all wash away as the God given right of respect is returned to the person who took heroin or other substances to overcome emotional or physical pain. This nurturing process helps the person to heal. Reiki works in this way, the healer manifests a channel between the universal love and the creator depending on which spiritual being you believe in. The seventh layer of the aura is connected to the crown chakra. This is the integration of both spiritual and physical i.e. mind, body and soul.

Doctor's are busy people. They are human with large mortgages, families, school fees, holidays-all the trapping of our modern world. They are trapped like ourselves in a merry go round of responsibilities. They have the same bank managers, are inflicted with emotions and stress, suffer anxiety, bad health from overwork, have marriage breakdown, may have to move, a host of similar complaints as the next (Joe Blog). We may go to the doctor with the hidden shame of abuse. The five or ten minutes that this people's helper can give you, turns into a nice pen writing a prescription for some antidepressants.

My own experiences of attending a doctor with recurring symptoms of stomach pain over a four year period was to be informed it was my imagination. Only when my father took a photograph of my skin and bones physical condition reminding me I resembled someone from a concentration camp was I persuaded to change doctors. The result was I had ceoliac disease for years. A change of diet was all that was needed. That gentle man could have saved me year of having needles containing morphine being stuck into my arse if he had used his grey matter and overlooked his textbook medical rules.

When even the medical professional old boys' network introduces new ways of interconnecting the aura, charkas, meditation, relaxation with their advanced medical knowledge we could see a breakthrough in a drop of prescription drugs and a lowering of chemical substances affecting the liver, neurotransmitters, receptors, bloodstream, glands which in turn can be responsible for depression, anxiety, fear, stress and other illness.

The aura expels different colours when we express different emotions or behaviours. If we are angry the aura will display a reddish yellow colour. Someone who snorts cocaine will have a grey colour from most of his nose to his head. The man or woman who has experimented with LSD shall have a pale grey tinted with green. A Reiki healer shall have a green aura about her head and shoulders. The person who plays music has wide aura of light yellow.

When I lecture on something I love which is how chemicals affect our health, I experience a bluish yellow colour before my eyes. If I am performing Reiki I send a pink healing from my heart as a means of opening my energy channels.

Someone holding emotion shall have a greyish chakra like a cloud around their heart. Blockages in the aura show up as dark colours. Physical diseases also display this colour. Those abusing heroin have a large swirling grey cloud about their whole body. Because most heroin abusers have past life trauma, it can take a few sessions to clear the aura. Crystals are a great source for this purpose. Individuals who absorb nothing but processed junk food can be seen to have a depleted aura.

This could be the result of the many chemicals that are ingested into the body. When a baby is born it has a high blue energy field around it. As it grows it must conform to society's limitations.

Sometimes children who have difficulty with this process shall develop a little friend that they give a name to. We are said to be reincarnated spirits, sent to complete our cycle of life. A child has an open energy field. He is vulnerable to his caregivers. Children have a great imagination; they are a clean slate until they reach a certain age. The little darling is devoid of a protective shield around his aura or charkas. Whenever a child seeks comfort from its parents, it could be that they are protected by the fields of which every parent is nurturing it at a given time. This is most noticeable with separation anxiety, which some children experience on attending their first school day. The young child shall carry a favourite toy, blanket for emotional comfort. It is its prized loved possession. It is part of the child. Today parents attend the first week at school with the child as they become accustomed to the mother leaving and returning. This reassuring behaviour reassures the child it is safe. Some teachers are not emotionally tuned into the child's feelings. It is these controlling individuals that shall grab the child, pushing the mother through the classroom door with the words "He'll be fine". It is just this reaction little Declan or Jill shouldn't be subjected to as the child learns to perceives that the school is a safe environment, where they can interact and play with new found friends, under the stern gaze of their new adult teacher.

As we saw in earlier chapters, the Lord of the Glands is the pituitary gland located at the back of the head. This secretes hormones that cause changes in the tests and ovaries. The dreaded adolescence has arrived. The home is infused with razor blades, underarm perfume (which is laced with alcohol), new clothes. The lazy sod has become the budding teenager intent on raining his new found confidence on the household. Music blasts off the doors, pictures of his favourite group are stuck to beautiful painted walls until only a fraction of blue or pink is visible.

What the parents don't see is that the energy field also changes. Private space is demanded as the growing teen seeks solitude from his siblings, and the old man. Hormones are running amok.

The adolescent feels vulnerable; his need to fit in can almost overwhelm him or her. Love flitters through the veins like a gushing river. Because the adolescent has no coping skills, these were done previously by his caregivers, the young individual is at sea when confronted with a problem, most likely he shall have no experience in coping skills and shall allow emotion to enter the frame.

If for example, they are anxious about a problem and are worried, they become apprehensive, frightened,

Depending on previous feedback, the strategies witnessed firsthand at home are the ones usually used to solve the problem and as some parents consume alcohol to get their minds off a problem the teenager may assume it is correct to do like-wise. Some vent anger while others seek emotional help from friends. Negative emotions cause blockages to the body stopping energy from flowing as it should. The budding adolescent will see alcohol or drugs as a means of shutting out the problem. Denial means we don't have to face reality.

Life experiences are what shape us, they help us grow. If we have a series of bad experiences we can go into negative freefall, blaming all around us for our misfortune. We give up our choice, the choice to take back our control. I often hear mothers complaining about having young adults still living at home. But these same mothers do their washing, refuse to take rent, make their dinner and put up with a dose of attitude that would send a monk into a lifelong retreat for some head space.

These well intentioned mothers are driven by a lack of fulfilment in their own lives. Their need to hold onto the twenty nine or thirty three year old son only makes that individual dependent, devoid of the personal development of a mature adult. It is something similar refusing to leave them at school. The mother's emotional need is greater than the child's, they can't let go.

An independent individual is mature, they don't seek acceptance from others. They are fulfilled, content with themselves.

Individuals on Methadone or (green diesel) are dependent on a substance to feel alive.

Methadone keeps their charka closed. Reiki helps to open these charkas rebalancing blocked energy. High doses of methadone combined with alcohol, chemicals such as pollutants i.e. sugar, fast food, shelf life food all add to an already overworked liver. Reiki's inner healing establishes health and balance because it focuses on emotional, physical, mental and spiritual aspects of the individual. When the Reiki healer lays his or her hands on the individual they channel the energy to the areas of the body that need repairing. The exercise leaves the person feeling a sense of worth, giving themselves unconditional love, they release old methods of blame, fear, anxiety by dispelling old traumas, which started them on a downward spiral of despair, only when they begin to learn alternative methods of coping, do they come to the conclusion that old outworn ways of dealing with problems was holding them in the grip of drugging.

Food glorious food

We get our energy from food, the nutrition that we eat each day in order to fuel our body. Many forms of energy surround us light, sound, heat, chemical, electrical and kinetic. Most of these play a role in our body. Muscles use chemical energy obtained from the food we eat to produce kinetic energy, movement and heat. The retina of the eye conveys energy to move electrical impulses which allows us to see.

Energy is measured in units called calories or joules. Carbohydrates and protein provide (four Kael per gram) fats provide (9 Kael per gram). Our metabolism which is a collective, chemical processes that breaks down complex substances into simpler ones which is known as catabolism. This releases energy needed to keep the body functioning. When the body is resting it is knowas a basal (a local metabolic rate). The (BMR) Basal Metabolic Rate increased when we sufferstress, fear, exertion and illness. This (BMR) is controlled by various hormones such as thyroxin,adrenaline (epinephrine) and insulin. Children who have inherited defects of body chemistry imbalance, that is errors of metabolism are caused by gene defects, this leads to abnormalfunctioning of an enzyme. Tay-Saches disease phenylketouria are reported to be due to this phenomenon. New born babies have blood taken from their following birth in order to detectphenylketonunia.

Food is broken down and stored as chemical energy in (ATP) molecules. This energy is available for energy which allows muscles contractions. Muscular activity and growth comes from the breakdown of carbohydrates, fats and proteins from the foods we eat or drink. We need energy to maintain our heartbeat, lungs and body temperature. All movement such as exercise, stress, increased energy expenditure. When we eat more than the body needs for energy it is store as surplus fat causing weight gain.

Our liver is the largest organ of the body. It is in the upper right abdominal cavity. It has two lobes surrounded by the hepatic artery. This supplies the liver with oxygenated blood. The portal vein supply's nutrient rich blood.

The liver plays a vital role in our body. It produces and processes a wide range of chemical substances which include important proteins for blood. It also produces cholesterol and special proteins that help the blood to carry fats around the body. Liver cells secret bile. This removes waste products from the liver aiding the breakdown and absorption of the fats in the small intestine. It processes nutrients for use by our cells, while storing excess glucose as glycogen. It controls blood levels of amino acids which we need for building protein. It does this by converting too high a level of amino acids into glucose, proteins or urea (for excretion).One of the liver's most important functions is to clear the blood of drugs and chemical poisons by breaking them down for excretion into the bile. We see this with individuals who abuse alcohol or heroin, it causes metabolic disorder. Individuals must continue to ingest the substance because the body's natural chemicals (neurotransmitters) have been depleted leaving unfulfilled receptors (specialised cells).

Cocaine activates the chemical (neurotransmitter dopamine) causing changes in mood. Most antidepressant drugs are manufactured to work in manipulating the neurotransmitters in the brain. They do this because they block the receptors. In cocaine abuse for example antidepressants are used to block the central nervous system by reducing the craving for the substance.

In heroin abuse methadone is seen as stopping the craving for heroin as it blocks receptors that have been left unfulfilled due to depletion of the brain's natural chemical endorphin due to over use of heroin.

Individuals who abuse alcohol for many years or who indulge in weekend binging can suffer from liver damage. Their excessive alcohol consumption causes the formation of fat globules between liver cells or fatty liver.

Hepatitis (caused by alcohol) can become cirrhosis which can increase the risk of liver cancer. If the person abstains, the liver can be prevented from further damage. This also applies to people abusing heroin. Many heroin addicts suffer from hepatitis or (HIV). In order to mend the liver they should abstain from further drugging, that means all drugs except those needed to help the liver replenish itself. The cells in our body produce a protein in response to viral infection. It increases the activity of the killer cells that form part of our immune system. Individuals who have HIV or hepatitis can be given the artificially produced drug Interferon to treat hepatitis and C. this treatment does however have side effects such as fever, headaches, depression, dizziness, tiredness.

The aura or energy field is blocked by the many chemical substances that we force our bodies to endure on a daily basis. The pulsing dynamic energy becomes stagnated as it struggles to eradicate unhealthy substances from over- running its normal function of clear energy. For our body to give us the health we require we must oblige it by given it the respect it deserves. That means recognizing that what we eat affects the internal workings of the brain, organs, glands. The inviting fast meal stuffed with all kinds of everything may fill your stomach giving you instant gratification in the form of a contented belly. What you fail to see is that the urge to indulge yourself in high carbohydrates is the brains way of informing you that your serotonin is low and needs the quick fix to maintain normal levels so you don't go into depression.

Pins and needles

meridians

The old traditional Chinese medical way of treating people was to look at the life force of the individual presenting with an illness. They perceived that blocked energy could result in a lack of harmonious movement of energies which affected the person's well being and behaviour. They saw this (life force) energy flowing in defined pathways such as blood and the vascular system.

These pathways or (meridians) meaning juing-lus to go through or to connect must be cleaned of all stagnated energy if good health was to be maintained.

Acupuncture is the method of inserting fine needles into the meridians (channels) of the body these thin five channels are believed to carry chi or energy around the human body. Twelve of these are major and are related or connected to a specific organ. In western medicine these are the heart, lungs and kidneys. They also related to other aspects of the person both emotionally and physically. The spleen and stomach have special colours such as yellow or the third chakra which is associated with emotion, taste, tissue.

This practice of Chinese medicine is as old as father clock himself, five thousand years, if we go back in time to our own history we also see how we have lost the knack of determining which herbs our ancestors used in the treatment of certain illness. Rushes for example were renowned for healing, as was demonstrated when Red Hugh o Donnell escaped from the dreaded Dublin Castle as far back as 1591. On his arrival at Rory Me Guire's in Enniskillen His galloglasses laid he on a bed of rushes so his toes could be amputated Red Hugh having spent three days and nights laying low in the Wicklow Mountains hidden by the O Byrne. His doctor treating him with a concoction of primrose, nettle, and his secret brew of herbs.

Acupuncturist works in a similar fashion it is non intrusive no net work of chemicals are needed as the practitioner places the needles at points in the body of the twelve major meridians. The channel which runs from the centre of the back across the crown of the head (where the pituitary gland rests) and ends on the top lip has twenty eight acupoints. Twenty four points which run from the conception point starts at the centre front ending at the bottom lip. When there is a deficiency of energy needles are inserted to release the blockages allowing chi (life force) to flow naturally from the meridians. By manipulating these channels of both the governor and conception much needed chi is allowed to flow. All in all Chinese medicine works on each meridian (channel) being connected to a pain or organs while also having a corresponding colour this element of acupuncture is fast becoming the in thing as people seek out new and alternative ways of dealing with energy blockages caused by emotional issues and stress, anxiety, divorce, separation and drug addiction. This ancient practice offers a non drug alternative to treating disease and symptoms especially pain. By unblocking stagnated energy it works like Reiki allowing those receiving it to release pent up emotion and stress and to cure disease. Drug addiction is sometimes described as a disease but many diseases can be cured by other drugs. Over a period of time evidence shows that individuals can detox from heroin if they are under a doctor's supervision and in a safe environment. The withdrawal symptoms of vomiting, cramps, dizziness, cravings if they can be endured lasts for a short period of time. When the heroin abuser attends counselling, gets support and is given life skills such as work experiences, computer skills, education they are more likely to cope with the stressful demands of survival. According to scientific theory acupuncture releases endorphins, the body's natural painkillers. The Chinese believe that the disconnection of body, mind and soul causes disease in the body. We are not separated from the mind, the brain and body central nervous system endocrine system all work like a giant computer sending and receiving chemical messages from and to cells, hormones.

When our mind is troubled these messages are transmitted to the glands which in time inform hormones that are released into the blood stream. Emotional and mental stress affects organs. We see this with ulcers and stress or worry is reported to be the main culprit for this condition. Stress has been proven to be the major link to heart attack. Acupuncture works because it restores imbalance in the energy system. Reiki also resolved energy imbalance, it channels life force to the area that has blocked energy.

Stress is an interference that disturbs a person's mental and physical wellbeing. When the body is faced with long periods of stressful situations it responds by increasing the production of adrenalin and cortical which causes changes in the heart rate, blood pressure and metabolism. When these reach a certain level they disrupt our ability to cope. A continued exposure to stress can lead to symptoms such as anxiety, depression, indigestion, palpitation, aches and pains. We see this in post traumatic stress when diazepam or some other sedative is prescribed to relieve these symptoms, when a relaxing treatment like acupuncture, Reiki, or reflexology, a good walk, and positive support could help the person deal with the issue of stress.

Imbalances, deficiencies, of certain vitamins or minerals can interrupt the natural workings of the body, if for example a builder didn't have the lintels to hold up the windows of his new building, it would collapse, he must have the proper equipment if the building is to be safe. The same applies to our body; we have an inherited set of genes which must undergo thrashing whenever we pump dangerous substances into it. Like the house without its lintels it will eventually crumble.

Unless we come to the realisation that we can stop the drug drain on the brain, body, liver, glands, we are on a hiding to nothing, it is only a matter of time until we see another generation of drug induced younger's handling stressful situations with dangerous chemicals. The blame can only lay at our door as we fail to react to the selective listening concerning alternative treatments as some of those in the medical profession stick their heads in the shit heap of despair by placing needles in areas around the ears, and certain aucpoints in the body this releases blockages allowing the methadone user to come to terms with their problems.

Silence is golden

The person who abuses substances is said to do so as a means of reliving tension, fear, worry, anger, emotional pain and sexual abuse. Stressful situations produce emotional reaction. Frustration is a common source of displaced aggression. Could the individual who abuses heroin, cocaine, or prescribed sedatives, barbiturates have displaced aggression that when social goals are blocked by the lack of education, dysfunctional parenting, alcoholic, abusive parents, poverty, homelessness abuse their aggressive drive is internalised so they hurt themselves by continuous use they drop into a physical spiral of unfilled receptors, chemical overload and a meltdown of human morals. Heroin abusers indulge in the strong opioid to block out pain. Is that pain at society, authority, family, hopelessness, despair? We cannot as an individual attack authority because society is Government, courts Garda, parents, school, and church.

When society does not provide alternative ways of coping with stress, or anxiety other than racing to the doctor or chemists shop for relief of pain, what are the alternatives? Meditations a natural high, it slows heart beat, it can re-energise your life, as you deal with the daily round-about of methadone taking, by stilling the mind, stopping the cowboy from cashing the Indians, around your head as you try to find solutions to an ever increasing unsolvable problem. Whenever you are in a meditative state you have taken control of your life, it is you and you alone that are stopping the rehash of doubtful thoughts, that beat you up with a mallet as you struggle to re -juggle the onslaught.

The daily toil of live for someone on methadone is like someone living behind net curtains- They can see what is going on around them but they are zapped of energy due to the drossy effect that the medication has on the nervous system. To add insult to injury they smoke and inhale nicotine a substance that works on the same premise as cocaine and heroin as it depletes dopamine the neurotransmitter much needed to stave off returning to the original source of all their problems.

Meditation allows you to view your life from a distance, to recognize that you belong to no one but yourself. That you are a spiritual being that has become caught in a web of drugs. Its techniques allows the individual to look within, to become aware that you have carried many an energy vampire in the form of family, friends, partners, teachers, society, and pharmaceutical companies, as you disappear into the beautiful rose where you are safe to indulge your-self without fear. That soul destroying thug that has clung to your chest crippling your advancement in the world. The gentle exercise of meditation is like an actor it allows you to escape into your own worlds you melt into safety without overloading your body on chemicals. You become a whirlpool of positive energy advancing at a safe pace as you gain strength to face reality. You can laugh, dance, whirl, and jump in your memories eye, as the child you were not allowed to be. Harsh criticism can be banished to the winds as you let all your fears, worries lag behind you like a kite, allowing each fear to drop off the face of the earth. Meditation if done on a daily basis can become spontaneous; it can make you pulsate with laughter, making your belly roll like the laughing police man. It knows no boundaries, it cannot hurt you like drugs, and it renews your spirituality the one thing drugging robs from you. It does not judge, comment, blame, condemn. It is tremendously simple once you master it. It has the same essence as a detox as it gets rid of the garbage that has built up over the years.

A simple think such as breathing can help you transcend time and space and won't cost a penny. Unlike heroin where the buss costs a fortune and lasts a short time. By listening to your breath as you eat, walk, and sit, you become alert to the workings of the body. Respect is given as you. Focus on a particular object, I use a pot of flowers, keep you're back straight and you eyes closed, breath deep into your belly. And as you do concentrate on the object, don't worry if you become distracted, this is normal at the beginning. Just go with the flow and allow the mind to wander until you feel ready to continue, this is the ego's way of refusing to release you. Pull you mind back like a piece of string, and start over. Remember all the time you are controlling this. As the meditation becomes second nature you can watch in amazement at the changes in your thinking, the empowerment you receive from meditation allows you to release negative thinking, criticism that has been instilled in you as a child. The battlefield between the ego and self will disappear taking you from a dark place to a warm place of light. Sorrow shall abandoned you as you let positive thoughts in, drugs are blinkers, they stop you from growing, they make other people wealthy, they keep communities in employment, the methadone taker exchanges one drug for another in their quest for peace and growth, but growth comes at the price of an overloaded liver, years of looking and acting like a legalised heroin addict. Meditation on the other hand shakes the individual out of the rut of fear, anxiety, apprehension; it gives its user unconditional love for them.

They can see beyond heroin and methadone as objects of relieve. I help to instil beauty of reality without drugs.

Meditation discharges the negative side of the ego, dependence, it replaces fear, it compensates for aloneness, it converts imbalance something a kin to acupuncture, and it has liberating effect on the person who has held unto their drugs like a comfort blanket for security.

Most of all it allows the return of spiritually experience, that they can cling unto as they find

Their reality in today's world.

Flowing River

Reiki

Reiki is the new kid on the alternative block of connecting the body, mind and soul. This exercise of hand positions which transfers healing energy from the giver to receiver is an old Japanese method of "ray-key" meaning universal life force.

Energy is allowed to flow from giver to receiver and goes to wherever it is needed to unblock energy in the person receiving it. This can occur on an emotional, mental, physical or spiritual level.

Those who practice Reiki like the old Chinese method of acupuncture the source of health is inner harmony. This ancient healing method is fast catching on as people seek holistic means of dealing with stressful situations and illness in their lives. Reiki is no great secret or magic? It can be learned by anyone who is open up to it. It promotes wellbeing and the receiver can receive positive effects on their life.

It replenishes energy, strengthens the immune system helping the person to fight disease. I have seen it dispel headaches without painkillers. Fear dissolves following a treatment. Symptoms are sent to show us that something is not functioning in the body. Reiki addresses this imbalance, it treats the body as a whole, and it relaxes and enriches one's life. It contributes to the renewal of energy to heal the physical and mental. This universal life force is what Reiki, it channels energy.

Reiki helps healing of all kinds, it relaxes pain both emotional and physical, and it also helps with spiritual growth. We saw in that last captive how stress has a crippling off effect on our physical and mental health. Our bodies show symptoms such as stomach pains, colds, and headaches. It lowers our immune system meaning the body needs more energy to fight infection. If we are stressed over a long period of time we develop diseases. Stress is a killer and Reiki deals with stress because it is a relaxation exercise lowing blood pressure and allowing the person to calm down.

Acupuncture, reflexology, meditation going for a peaceful stroll in the fresh air staying positive. All have a beneficial effect at relaxing the body, mind and lifting the spirit. Because Reiki strengthens the immune system we are more able to fight infection, flu's, cold, sores. It replenishes us allowing a build up of energy creating a healing body.

Reiki means "universal life force". The Japanese pronounce it "Rei-ki". All of life's creatures are bundles of energy. In India it is called panan. In Western society we call it light. The vegetables, flowers, plants, all live and breathe they do so because of cells and energy. The Reiki practitioner channels the energy through his hands to the recipient which then activates the body's natural ability to receive and heal it. I have seen this first hand in my dealings with substance abuser. It would take almost two years of counselling to break through the low self-esteem, defensive mechanisms, denial and lack of confidence or pain, where treatments with Reiki and crystals a breakthrough can come within six months or less. This safe holistic healing system is not done by me per say rather it happens due to the individuals opening up to be healed by unblocking old emotional hurts by letting go. By placing my hands on another person, their energy is drawn down (not by me) through me to the part of the body I touch. The problems afflicting the receiver such as asthma, stress, eczema, anxiety, fear, depression, insomnia can be addressed allowing the person to return to well-being.

While Reiki is an alternative healing system, it is not, and I do not advise anyone reading this to substitute orthodox medicine for Reiki. If you happen to suffer from a serious disease you should continue to attend your doctor or hospital. Prescribed drugs should not be discontinued and no Reiki practitioner would encourage a person to undertake such a decision. Reiki I find is good for emotional blocks. Especially suppressed feelings that have been carried like a worn out schoolbag that the person has buried in their unconscious. Sadness, neglect, hurt, anger, abuse, negative thoughts pounded into their heads by peers, family, teachers, society and church. Reiki helps the individual to own and forgive themselves, to let go of outworn attitudes in their effort to heal. It helps with the progression of moving forward, to take control of their lives, to accept responsibility for past mistakes. It helps the person receiving it to become aware both emotionally and mentally. It does this by relaxing both the mind and body, dissolves negative emotional hang-ups and belief about themselves. Spiritual growth is enhanced as the receiver opens up.

The Endocrine System and the charkas are believed to be interconnected by way of the endocrine system conveying energy to the charkas and vice versa. Energy is channelled to the body bringing balance.

The Endocrine System pituitary gland is connected to the Seventh Chakra.

The pineal gland is connected to the Sixth Chakra.

The Thyroid Gland is connected to the Fifth Chakra.

The Thymus is connected to the Fourth Chakra.

The Adrenal Gland is connected to the Second Chakra.

The Pancreas is connected to the Third Chakra.

The ovaries or testes are connected to the First Chakra.

The pituitary gland is the overall lord of the glands. This outgrowth of the brain lies below the hypothalamus. It controls the release of different hormones, while it also triggers the action of the Thyroid gland, the sex glands and the outer layer of the adrenal gland. Its relationship with the hypothalamus also has an effect on the interaction that takes place between the Endocrine System and the Nervous System. When we are stressed, emotionally upset; suffer from fear, pain or anxiety a substance called (CRE) is carried from the hypothalamus to the pituitary gland. This in turn stimulates the over lord of the glands to release the hormone (ACTH) into the bloodstream it is then grabbed from the bloodstream by receptors into the cells and releases other hormones. The adrenal gland is responsible for mood, our energy and ability to cope.

Adrenal glands inner core secretes adrenalin and noradrenalin. Adrenaline prepared the body for emergency or (fight or fright) by affecting the muscles and sweat glands. The heart beats faster. Noradrenalin stimulates the release of a hormone which acts on the outer part of the adrenal glands. This pair of small endocrine glands is located above the kidneys. The outer cortex is longer than the inner medulla.

The cortex secretes aldosterone with a few other hormones to help maintain blood pressure. Hydrocortisone controls the body's use of fat proteins and carbohydrates and is important in helping our body deal with stress. This hormone along with corticosterone suppresses some activities of the immune system. (ACTH) is produced by the pituitary gland. The adrenal medulla is part of the sympathetic autonomic nervous system. The release of nor epinephrine into the bloodstream activates the hormone that acts on the outer layer of the adrenal gland which in turn sends a second hormone to the liver to increase the sugar level so the body has energy for fast action. Hormones and neurotransmitters work in similar ways by carrying messages between cells of the body. While neurotransmitters job is to communicate messages between neurons, hormones have the task of travelling through the body.

The pituitary gland then is connected to the seventh chakra which is located as the site of the cerebral cortex. The sixth chakra in the human body is connected to the medulla oblongata, this lies below the skull, just above the spinal cord. The upper lungs are connected to the fifth chakra. The heart and lower lungs are connected to the fourth chakra. The liver, spleen stomach are all connected to the third chakra, as is the pancreas. The kidneys, small and large intestine and bladder are connected to the second chakra.

As we have seen the pineal gland is a cone shaped structure deep in the brain, its function is to secrete melatonin in response to changes in light. The thyroid gland is located in the neck or fifth chakra; it is one of the main endocrine glands. It helps to regulate the body's internal processes. It secrets T4 or Thyroxin hormone when this gland id disturbed it can result in over activity or under activity. Sometimes a genetic disorder results in the glands inability to secrete hormones, when this occurs goitre may appear. Hyperthyroidism is the result of an excess production of (TSH) by the pituitary gland. This can sometimes be caused if a pituitary tumour exists. Goitre is associated with a lack of iodine production, which is necessary for thyroid hormones. These hormones are T4, (T3) this regulates metabolism and calcitonin which helps to regulate calcium levels in the body.

The thymus gland is connected to the fourth chakra. This forms part of the immune systems we have already seen it is connected to the upper lungs and heart. Each lobe of the thymus is made up of lymphoid tissue. The Islets of langerhans in the pancreas is connected to the third chakra.

This organ lies across the back of the abdomen behind the stomach. It has both a hormonal and digestive function. It secrets enzymes and sodium bicarbonate which neutralises stomach acids entering the duodenum. It contains cells known as islets of langerhans which secrets insulin and glucagon's. It is these hormones that regulate glucose in the blood. Diabetes mellitus is a condition that occurs when not enough insulin is produced. Smoking, alcohol or a high intake of fats are said to contribute to pancreas cancer. This tumour of the exocrine tissue show themselves as abdominal pain loss of appetite, weight loss and jaundice, vomiting, tiredness, diarrhoea. The liver is also connected to third chakra. This plays a vital role in the body. It produces and processes a range of chemicals important proteins, cholesterol, it secrets bile which removes waste products from the liver and aids the breakdown of fats in the small intestine. It is the processing factory for which nutrients for call use. It stores glucose, controls amino acids. It cleans the blood of (drugs) toxins or poisons by breaking them down and excreting them via bile. The adrenal gland is connected with the second Chakra, the kidneys, small and large intestines.

These are above the kidneys producing two hormones following the release of (AETH) the bodies main stress hormone by the pituitary gland. The adrenal glands functions are to release over 30 hormones to help the body to deal with stress, coping. These hormones are adrenaline and noradrenalin which in turn affects the fast release of blood sugar for a quick fix of energy. The sex glands and ovaries in women or gonad in men. These secrete hormones necessary for reproduction. Ovaries produce the hormone oestrogen and progesterone. While the male organs produce testosterone. Energy that pulsates from these glands are said to be chemicals that attract, desire partnership, emotionally stability. If malfunctions occur either in the endocrine system, the neurotransmitters or receptors, nervous system the body can go into freefall.

Chemicals and hormones go haywire releasing too little or too much which in turn can affect the body causing illness. Neurotransmitters, the central nervous system, the endocrine system, somatic system the autonomic system are all interconnecting like a large spider's web sending and receiving chemical message. It is only natural to believe that any synthetic toxins, drugs, pesticides, insecticides that the human body inhales, absorbs, ingests, will interfere with this natural processing plan that is the human body.

Reiki is one of a number of alternative ways of releasing blocked energy. In doing so it permits the individual to come into contact with suppressed feelings of anger, fear, sadness, stress, unhappiness and a list of others that if not treated can cause illness physically or spiritually.

Reiki is an un-intrusive holistic treatment like acupuncture or reflexology it does not place chemicals into an already overloaded body. A body that must with-stand the onslaught of junk food, processed food with its sodium, artificial colouring or hormones that are fed to cattle, pigs, chickens. Even the good old cabbage must undergo the rigorous dousing of insecticides and pesticides so it can have a shinny fat belly as it displays its chemical freshness on a supermarket shelf. These shelves are displaying fresh fruit like tomatoes, grapes, strawberries, blueberries, apples, carrots and a host of other fruit or vegetables. Most of these are continental coming from shores such as Israel, Spain, Greece, Portugal, Holland and France. Like returning Vikings' they hurry by truck loads to reach our shops in their quest to invade and plunder our neurotransmitters, hormones and in then creep into our nervous system which then is swamped with prescribed drugs (chemicals) from the G.P.

Reiki was invented by Dr. Mikao Usui following his quest to find answers to study the healing methods of Christ. It was on this search that he encountered the works of Buddha another Holman who had lived in 600BC. Buddha taught meditation as he travelled throughout India and it is reported he could dispel disease by challenging energy to areas of the body that had become blocked by emotional issues. This holy man like Christ possessed the power of healing. He did not do the healing instead opened himself up spiritually so the powers that be could channel energy through him.

Dr. Usui found symbols and mantras in old ancient writings of Buddha. It is these that are the key to Reiki healing. After spending long periods in a Buddhist monastery he undertook a twenty one day meditation. Remember Christ fasted and mediated as did Moses and Mohammad. As the symbols and mantras became clear to the doctor he believed he had received a healing force. On leaving the holy mountain he hurt his toe that resulted in pain and bleeding. Holding his hands about his damaged foot the pain vanished, leaving no sign of injury. This spiritual experience prompted him to work with the poor and sick. After spending seven years of doing so he was faced with the dilemma that while he could heal the physical diseases of the poisoned body he needed to heal the overall body emotionally, mentally, spiritually. That his desire to help and heal needed to be fuelled by the individual desire for complete healing. The person who received the healing needed to give something back in order to give something back in order to feel cherished, whole. It has to be an exchange of energy (life force) for the healing to have an overall effect on the individual's wellbeing.

On Dr. Usui's death his successor A. Drtteyashi opened a Reiki clinic. He left documents pertaining to how Reiki finds the cause of physical symptoms it does this by filling the body with required energy needed to restore health. Following a series of high profile healings, Reiki has become world renowned with many Reiki masters. In countries such as Spain, Italy, America, Canada, England, Sweden, Australia, Asia and Africa Reiki is now used to treat some cancer victims.

Tibetan monks believe that our healing channels can vibrate to transfer energy. Mantras and symbols increase the vibration sequence of the body. Because the mantra is non-verbal or a thought wavelength, it creates a vibration, it is something like telepathy.

We see this with music and sound it is vibration. Music can be received by the chakras or energy centres. Our energy channels are like waste pipes, they can become blocked, contaminated with chemicals or pollutants. It must be kept clear and clean otherwise the water shall become stagnated and bacteria or toxins shall gather. Reiki works in a similar way; it unblocks the channels allowing the flow of chi or life force.

Simulate My Nerve Endings

Reflexology works by applying pressure on the feet and hands. By mapping the feet's reflex zones in which a certain point of the human foot corresponds to certain

Organs in the body, something similar to acupuncture except it is not needles but fingers. Like Reiki and Acupuncture, reflexology's is searching for energy blocks which is now believed to cause illness, by using certain hand movements they seek to release these built up blockages. Like Reiki reflexology once learned can be self administered.

The top of the large toe is said to represent the brain. Underneath the big toe at the fat part is the pituitary gland. The area running along the side of the outside big toe represents the nose and mouth. Further down is the heart while the heart, lungs is situated near the centre middle, below the big toe. The pancreas, kidneys, small intestine are situated further down the inside of the foot. The toe next to the large toe is associated with the head; the two beside it are to do with sinuses. The pressure points for the eyes, ears are located under the small toe and the one next to it. Feet are what keep us mobile. We move from A to Z on a daily basis. It is the one area of the body that individuals neglect. There is nothing better than soaking two sore feet in a warm bubble tub as the water vibrates around and over them placing a few drops of essential rose oil in a tub of water.

Touch is physical contact, it conveys to the receiver tenderness, causing love an expression of emotion. When we watch lions, dogs, wolf, cats, goats, horses or other animals they lick, smell, sniffing, this daily contact is their attempt at social interaction and grooming. As babies and children we are touched, kissed by our caregivers. This powerful experience allows us to feel secure to explore as we take our first steps in the knowledge that strong hands hold us if we fall. Studies show that touch and tender handling is crucial for the healthy, emotional, physical and mental development.

When a child stumbles, or has an accident the mother's touch can stop the tears, smooth the hurt, stroking a hot forehead is known to bring down a temperature. As seen in the previous chapter touch can heal. Christ healed by laying his hands on the person. Touching someone is essential for calming their nerves and relieving stress. Dogs and cats are now considered a powerful tool in the healing process of elderly or cancer patients. It is reported that stroking a cat or dog can bring down blood pressure.

This chapter deals with the ancient therapy of head massage. This technique is a powerful stress buster and is carried out in most hair salons. Having the scalp gently rubbed can dispel headache as you unwind from a stressful lifestyle.

This therapy is deemed to work very well on those suffering from drug addiction, insomnia, stress and migraines. Those suffering from depression are also reported to benefit. This wonderful, relaxing therapy fast becomes as popular as Reiki as people seek solutions to popping pills in their effort at coping with a hectic life. By working on an emotional and physical it helps to relieve the build up of tensions, gives a feeling of comfort and belonging. The person receiving Indian Head Massage can be acquainted with the healing potential of their inner self discovering balance and uniqueness. Touch is a universal language. Rubbing, holding, pressing, touching is as natural as washing one's face or hands. Unfortunately as we grow from children to adults, we are expected to grow up, become adults, become independent. Touch is lost somewhere in-between teenage years and only resurfaces when we meet someone and fall in love, intimacy got lost along the way. We are taught to deal with situations in the same way our parents dealt with difficulty. We are not taught to deal with stress, how to cope, and fear feelings of failure. We are not given unconditional love but are judged and given love when we fulfil the needs or expectations of our parents, loved ones, peers, society. When we develop an illness, the people help us prescribed pills, we are informed to pick one up, get a grip, or snap out of depression. The daily grind of pressure, traffic jams, uncertainties, unemployment, loss, divorce are seen as normal, a part of one's life, survival. But evidence shows that stress does kills, cause illness, continued over long periods it can break down the immune system.

Most stress is not negative. Stress can also stimulate us by motivating us to do something about our daily life. An example it could be that the individual who is stressed out sitting in a two hour traffic jam and decides that to eliminate stress, he can work from home. We saw how hormones are released from the adrenal glands (adrenalin) to deal with the threat of fear, emotional problems. These responses can be harmful if they are not dealt with in an appropriate manner. When we feel we have no control over a given situation or one frustrated by our circumstances, perhaps because we are bullied at work by an insecure boss. We may want to leave the job but because of bills, children, mortgage, no skills we may frustrated internalising this anger in a negative way, believing we have no control and therefore can see no way out.

Human beings have a tendency to focus on the negative. Our attentions drawn to weakness, we become pessimistic, worry about the future when the present moment is all we have. Change can be traumatic for anyone moving house. Difficult relationships play havoc with our emotions sending us diving for the nearest pub as we panic at the thought of separation. Single mothers trying to raise children in very difficult circumstances an environment flushed with drugs, danger, aggression, dissatisfaction. Single fathers can often suffer stress over continuous control issues around getting to see their children or who is replacing them in the ex partner's life. Ill health in the family or the death of a mother or sister by suicide or an overdose of drugs.

Events that are positive also cause stress, getting married, having a baby are life changing events. The previous chapters dealt with now the body works by receiving signals from the nervous system via our senses this triggers the hypothalamus to send messages to the pituitary gland adrenalin is released to the bloodstream to help the body deal with the emergency. The functioning mechanisms is disrupted as blood pressure rises the heart beats faster, breathing becomes shallow and rapid. Prolonged stress has the result of diverting much needed resources to deal with the stress. Cholesterol raises anxiety, indigestion, palpitations, depression, aches and pains. The individual's ability to cope is affected as concentration is, disturbed. The individual who abuses harmful substances lives a continuous stressful existence, days of trying to feed their heroin habit, sleeping rough, robbing, fear of physical assault, rape, and loss of family, HIV, hepatitis and a host of other dangers. The daily stresses can break down the immune system causing other illnesses such as irritable bowel syndrome, Chrone's disease, pancreatic and heart attacks. As mentioned in the previous chapter the pancreas is located in the islets of langerhans which are connected to the third chakras. This very important organ is vital for good health.

Most of us don't know we are stressed until some physical symptom presents itself. Sweating, muscular tension, shallow breathing, loss of interest in sex, no appetite, diarrhoea, insomnia, constipation and worse ulcers. Emotions are disrupted also. Frustration, anxiety, mood swings, wanting to escape, panic attacks, feeling helpless, low self-esteem, confusion, phobias, forgetting, no sense of humour. The body is out of balance. It has lost homeostatic. Reiki, Indian head massage, meditation, reflexology, acupuncture all have a beneficial effect on restoring the body's balance.

The individual receiving these hands on pampering shall feel safe and confident. Because Indian Head Massage stimulates the blood and works the lymphatic system, it can help to drain toxins from the body. Methadone users do appear to benefit greatly, mainly because they feel cherished and cared for but above they are not judged nor ask to change their individuality. They are not made to feel different, like lepers just because they have chosen a different path to what society deems correct for them. Methadone is acceptable it is approved by the government and therefore by society but the differences between these two resembles a spiders web, it is so thin you hardly notice the spider until you are trapped struggling and panting until you accept that you have been duped. Individuals who abuse substances on a daily basis methadone are their only escape route from a life of hell.

When holistic methods are intergraded into the treatment of those on this potent drug, one can see change take place before their eyes. Like Reiki, Indian head massage works on centre points on the head

Relaxing the scalp, allowing the natural production of oil to flow, by stimulation circulation the head becomes warm, by nourishing the scalp it helps to drain toxins that have accumulated beneath the scull.

Our hair does hold toxins for long periods. Scientists cut hair whenever they need to test for arsenic poisoning. Because modern shampoo strips the hair from its natural oils, it also contains chemicals Shampoo made with organic pure soap is more suitable. Plucking and stroking intensify the relaxation; these techniques leave you with a sleepy feeling. Tapping and squeezing the head between the palms of the hands which releases tension or headaches caused by stress. Making circular movements at the temples stimulates blood flow, relieves eyestrain. Touch is a power tool against stress. A simple exercise such as twiddling the ears with the thumb or fingers can help relax the person you are touching. Our ears have nerve endings and because they are sensitive to touch, the sensation helps to distract the brain away from the problem that is causing you stress. Playing one's fingers across another's eyes also releases stress; the face suddenly relaxes giving a feeling of wellbeing. Next time you feel short tempered, or stressed out, light a green candle with a little rose oil, sit in a quiet spot and tickle your ears or better still place your hands on your solar plexus, breath in and out counting to three say "I live-in the moment". In the next chapter we shall look at meditation and how it can benefit those on methadone programme.

Stressed out of your scull

"An Old proverb says, "it's not what you Eat, but what's eating you"

Relieving stress can be one of the most difficult things to do. The more we fight to control situations around us the more difficult it becomes and the more stressful we become. Concentrating the mind is an arduous task if we are emotionally worked up, stressed, suffering from anxiety or pain and illness. If for example you are on one hundred mils of methadone each day, your concentration centres on your next visit, to receive your dose of green diesel. You can carry on with the day's tasks but individuals would become anxious if they discovered that the clinic had closed unexpectedly leaving them without their opinion. Concentration would most likely fly out the window to be replaced by fear, anxiety, and worry.

Meditation is not a practice where the individual performs deep breathing exercises that controls and regulates the person breath restricting their attention from the external and internal problems that they perceive they cannot solve nor have little control over. By regulating their breath they slow down their heart rate. Meditation has been practiced in Tibet, India and around the world. The individual achieves an altered state allowing them to relax both physically and mentally. Stressful situations cause emotional and physiological arousal, which in turn causes feelings of discomfort. The individual is forced to address the problem causing the stressor to accelerate which adds to further stress. Heroin abusers will tell you that they became stress out of their skull when they had no fix. Confusion accompanies stress like a pair of best friends. In order to diffuse the stressor it must be identified first. Heroin gives its user instant gratification; it dispels pain, anxiety, stress. The dark alleyway or shop doorway is less threatening when one is drugged up on heroin. The abuser has gained control over his miserable existence for the moment anyhow. He or she is able to cope with one fix at a time. Most heroin addicts do not have problem coping skills; they usually use emotion to deal with their problem, stress, death, loss of parent through separation. Substance abusers will tell you they consume alcohol, inject heroin or sniff cocaine as a means of stopping stress, pain, and depression due to the fact they feel like failures and are treated as such by those around them. Their problems appear to overwhelm them sending them rushing for the method they know best to shut out the hurt. We all deal with problems in our own way. The breakdown of a marriage of a friend will send the person running to a best girlfriend to discuss the "bastard" of a husband. Men deal with emotion differently. Some do talk to a good mate while others address their hurt ego by joining the lads in a drinking session to release the tension pretending to be the strong man that we expect them to be. "Big boys don't cry"

Support is all important to the individual who is going through a personal trauma. This is evident especially among methadone programmes. The rehabilitation of the addict into the community is geared towards skills education, self development, and self awareness and counselling. Support is available when needed. The individual attends on a daily basis to the centre and receives a wage, something that enables the building of self esteem and independence.

School education does not inform us how to solve problems unless it is to do with mathematics or exams. The problems that occur every day in everyday life are left at the school gate as the pupil departs for home. Studies carried out by an American University on a group of students showed that individual who use drugs, or alcohol tend to remain depressed following a bereavement, or suicide they returned to old habits to gain a sense of control, and were more unlikely to cope. Those students who took up another activity, going for a walk, working out or doing another form of distraction to lift their mood. This is an interesting point because it focuses on why some of those taking methadone remain on this green diesel for sometimes up to ten years. They become dependent on a system of past coping skills to relieve them of the stress and emotion associated with hurt, loss, or feeling alone in the world. Lack of coping skills holds them prisoner as similar as if they were still behind bars. Of course another important issue we should never over-look is the lack of money to move outside their deprived environment where most methadone takers reside. "One cannot buy a silk purse with a pig's ear."

When we address the real issues around continuous drugging or educate those on fat wages who make decisions about real lives but are cocooned in an area far removed from boy racers, breaking windows as children sleep, where misguided loyalty means "do to them before they do it to your family". Where moving away from your area or family means facing separation anxiety on a grand scale because the family are all you know, and who gives you a pull out until you receive next week's dole.

Meditation of one of the best mood lifters one could engage in when stabilising methadone the individual achieves a calm minds, one devoid of worry. By exhaling and inhaling the individual is using the pain to concentrate and focus on a particular object (breath). The deep breathing technique can bring clarity causing the excitement of the brain to still itself. By focusing, the brain we can stop the stressors from interruption for a few seconds. The heaviness of the mind and body can prevent clarity and intense mind needs to be loosened like loosening the springs of a violin, too tight and the strings break. The mind also needs to be tuned like a stringed instrument. When an individual develops concentration they become skilled in dealing with thoughts calming them and are therefore able to deal with one problem at a time.

The calm feeling obtained by practising meditation can produce an alertness and clarity that no amount of drugging could produce and it is one less chemical for the overworked liver to absorb. Because concentration is an essential part of meditation it takes a while to get used to but is achievable with continuous practicing.

By visually seeing an object before you, you can focus on that object alone. I usually see a vase with one white lily simply because I like lilies. I exclude everything else in the room, feelings, sounds or sensations. The vase should fill your visual field. A mantra can be chanted as sound is energy. This sound can help induce a calm relaxed feeling. The muscles of our body should be relaxed as you concentrate on your breathing. With practice you should improve the technique. The meditation not only helps you to relax it can induce a feeling of peace. Those abusing heroin shall say the drug gave them a peaceful feeling, it shut out the world. The benefits of meditation are important for those abusing drugs. It induces physiological arousal, induces relaxation having the same effect as heroin. It decreased oxygen consumption, lowers heart rate, stabilises blood flow, but most important of all it decreases cortical arousal reducing mental activity. It stills the mind, stops it from racing. It is also reported to help with anxiety. The question remains, one that we need to ask. If a natural method of changing the brain waves, helps anxiety, relieves stressors, appears to have a similar action as heroin. It induces sleep, calms nervous system, blocks out anxiety, emotional problems, and lowers both blood pressure and rate which is to do with metabolism, why oh why are doctors and medical practitioners not using alternative methods to help their patients come off drugs? Does it make sense to stabilise someone on heroin with opium, or to treat someone who suffers from anxiety with a Valium. Drugs that are chemicals that interfere with the body's natural balance.

Methadone is a toxin, alcohol is a toxin, Valium is a toxin, and pollutants are toxins. The most professional sports men and women in the world use meditation as a means of concentration and success. Sports psychologists use this method for preparing their clients for efficiency in their game. Why then are we as a society not doing the same for those in society who need our help on the road to independence? Manufacturing the white power from the hot sunny climate to the laneway of a city street can make a profit on the misery of those who have very little life skill or coping skills. Coping is surviving in what way you can. Individuals who enter methadone programmes show progress when they receive support, and counselling, have an opportunity to receive education and skills that can reinvent their life allowing them to fit back into society. They are helped to take control of their lives the so called disease that has plagued them for most of their teenage years. Disease according to conventional medicine is a pattern of tests, symptoms that lead to a diagnosis of a disease. Chinese maintain that disease is the result of physical, emotional, spiritual, mental imbalance.

Drug addiction is emotions that one suppressed, negative thinking, low self-esteem, lack of confidence, fear, anxiety about the future. Evidence exists that meditation reduces physiological arousal. The individual who suffers from pain, negative emotions, emotional pain, stress and anxiety, is the taking of heroin, methadone, Valium, sedatives and other drugs a coping mechanism? Does the heroin strengthen self -confidence, help emotional coping? Heroin according to individual who abuse this powerful drug shuts out pain. Is this aforesaid memories of neglect, abuse, guilt or shame, low self-esteem, failure in education system or are we dishing out methadone to keep repressed failure from rising from the seabed like the Titanic. As a society are we projecting our own undesirable traits, ones like alcohol, smoking blame on to those who do drugs. Projection is an unconscious mechanism; it protects us from recognising undesirable qualities by assigning them to other people. If we can pass the buck by telling ourselves that methadone keeps down crime rates, is economical, that the abuser of heroin gets what the deserve then we don't have to look anywhere else. That it is more addictive than heroin is big bucks to those dealing or manufacturing it and a whole industry thriving because people who lack emotional coping skills perhaps the individual left school without any qualifications, is unemployable, has taken a forced vacation at the expense of the tax payer at one   of our finest goals where they can get their drug of choice at the drop of a hat, drugs needed physically to fill the unfulfilled receptors that heroin or other drugs have depleted. His daily fix of white power sniffed, injected, or smoked, ensures he or she does not vomit, have uncontrolled shaking, stomach cramps, or the other ailments associated with withdrawals.

Self care is essential for survival for relationships. Independence builds self confidence, when we are confident we feel that we have achieved, therefore we fit in. We are accepted. Self care is not selfish, it is not self indulgent. In order for a wolf to maintain its cubs it must hurt, kill to survive.

Those who indulge in the abuse of substances are riddled with guilt, shame; they cannot see the wood for the trees. Methadone programmes while helping to stabilise the individual, also prolongs their dependency on drugs or others. If someone is given daily handouts they don't' have to set themselves the choice of doing something about their predicament. We see this in the welfare state. It is easier to become dependent on two hundred euro per week as a single person, to receive rent allowance of anything up to eight hundred a month, plus free medical care, hospital care, school clothes. Why would they contemplate working? This spiral of dependency robs them of their self worth, respect, pride. They live a lifetime on the treadmill of dependency. Live in dependent communities, where the norm is learned helplessness and perhaps go on to raise another generation of children who believe that everyone owes them a living.

Meditation is similar to heroin in that the person achieves an altered state; all problems are blocked out while they concentrate on their breathing. Problems are also blocked out by the drug as in antidepressants, cocaine or stimulants. The perceived change in mood allows the user to shut down emotionally, they wave good to stress ,their adrenal gland takes a vocation, as they slumber in a coma of blissfulness, they know their high is always available.

Methadone provides the same effects as heroin; it differs only in that the individual is assured of its availability. Unlike his or heroin habit where they have to finance it personally, methadone is provided free by the state government. Methadone is dangerous if taken with alcohol or cocaine. The already damaged liver is piled with more chemicals, as it struggles to cope with (HIV) or hepatitis. Junk food pollutants, insecticides, Tran-fats, medication, caffeine, nicotine, processed food and water laced with chlorine. This liver overload results in skin blemishes, high blood pressure, high cholesterol, indigestion and insomnia.

The liver is one of the most important organs in the human body. One of the main functions is fat metabolism. Bile is separated by the liver and stored in the gallbladder. This in turn breaks down fats. For the bile to do a proper job it needs certain nutrients that if these are not available the bile becomes thickened by chemicals, toxins, drugs and metals. Methadone, heroin, antidepressants, stimulants, processed food, junk food, household items, gas, oil, water all contain certain chemicals alcohol, coffee and nicotine. The liver has two pathways which eliminate or break down toxins in the body. We take these toxins into our body either by ingestion; absorb it through our skin, senses or up our noses. Prescribed drugs we ingest, pollutants we can smell and take in on vegetables, fruit, oils. This red-brown structure with its hepatic artery that supplies oxygenated blood to the liver with its brother the portal vein supplies nutrient rich blood. This deoxygenated enters into the hepatic vein where a network of ducts carries the bile from the liver to the gallbladder.

The liver's role is to produce and process chemical substances such as protein for the blood. Cholesterol and special proteins carry the fats around the body. Bile secreted from liver cells removes waste products from the liver while aiding the breakdown and absorption of fats in the small intestine. This great overworked organ processes nutrients for use by the cells in our body. It controls the blood level of amino acids which is the building blocks of proteins; it converts this into glucose, proteins, if the levels are high.

By cleaning the blood of chemicals and toxins which are excreted in the bile. If someone has a liver abscess it can be the result of an intestinal infection spread by bacteria. Cirrhosis of the liver is damaged caused by excessive alcohol consumption. Hepatitis this is inflammation of the liver which damages cells. It is transmitted in the blood or other body fluids, sharing needles, sexual contact. The symptoms may include fever, headache, and jaundice. Acute hepatitis can be the result of an infection. It can also be the result of exposure to alcohol, toxic chemicals or drugs. So what are we pumping into young and not so young people. Drugs. Methadone is a drug, cousin of heroin. It is more addictive with individuals having to take this green diesel for many years. Pesticides are chemicals sprayed on the shiny carrots, cabbage, tomatoes, wheat, herbs, beans, peas, flowers. All and everything we place in our mouths are sprayed for economic benefit, profit and greed. A human is measured in Euros. The question first asked is "How much shall it cost". Compare why methadone is given instead of heroin. It is more cost efficient, it keeps down crime rates. What is not said is that because this jungle juice lasts twenty four hours to Mr Heroin's expensive three or four. Takeaways are given at weekends, no need to pay73 overtime as those availing of this green monster scuttle to replenish their much needed drug, they are not aware of the build up of this drug in their overworked liver. Whenever this vital organ is overloaded with chemicals it cannot do its work, metabolic by-products of incomplete detoxification can build up in the body. Medication prescribed by many doctors to bring down cholesterol can in fact damage the liver which is responsible for making cholesterol in the first place. This fatty substance is an important constituent of body cells and hormones and the much needed bile salts for the liver. It is made by the liver from foods especially saturated fats, eggs. High blood cholesterol levels increase the risk of coronary artery disease or stroke. Cholesterol is influenced by diet to have an acceptable count of five means reducing saturated fats. Unfortunately the satins prescribed to bring cholesterol down such as Lipitor are toxins, as are some drugs and are reported to erode the marrow in the bone, cause cramps, and can affect liver function.

Drugs for treating some forms of arthritis also have a similar effect as stated on the package. Birth control pills are another culprit. Hormone replacement therapy and some herbs. What are we dumping into the methadone takers liver? This legally prescribed drug of eighty to one hundred and twenty mils per day ads up to taking the latter over one week that amounts to seven hundred and forty mills of methadone that the individual's liver must try to dispel. Taken over a month it adds up to 2,960 mills, multiply that by one year it would-be near 19,600 mills of green diesel that an already overloaded or damaged liver must process in its daily struggle at surviving. If we add all the junk food, chemicals, pollutants, fizzy drinks, power drinks, alcohol, nicotine, coffee, tea, to top all this we are presented with imported visitors in the form of meat or chicken from Holland, fruit and vegetables from Greece, Spain, Portugal, France keeping in mind that these countries do not have the same restrictions on chemical use as we do, then we have a liver crisis on our hands. If the bile is minus its much needed salts the individuals who don't feel the need to question what they are putting into their bodies may wonder why their use foods like the dimpled orange or why accumulated fat around their middle reminds them of the Michelin man on a bad day. Their apple shaped body may suddenly become watermelon shaped as their muscles work under the weight of a toxic liver, sluggish lymphatic system. If a garbage bin is overflowing it needs to be emptied otherwise it shall gather rats. We would not want that so we ensure we leave it out for collection. Whey then do we treat our liver so badly allowing others to dump chemicals, metals, processed food laced with chemicals, pesticides, cattle, sheep, poultry all dosed with antibiotics in the name of eradicating illness. The individuals who abuse heroin may see methadone as a safe alternative to his symptoms of withdrawal. The person who suffers from anxiety may see his or her salvation from the physical arousal when dumping the drug into their system. Heroin is a depressant, it shields its user from his terror, fear, shame, and limit learned helplessness. Withdrawal can result in brain excitation due to the unfulfilled receptors. The reasons that the abuser has started to use heroin returns with a vengeance. Anxiety, cold sweats, shaking as the neurotransmitter dopamine sets off unpleasant symptoms. Barbiturates, intoxication cause the person to slur his or her speech. These are broken down by the liver and passed via the kidneys.

According to (O'Brien and Cohen 1984) it is not known how these powerful drugs work on the neurotransmitters, only that the exciter neurotransmitters are impaired. An overdose of these drugs can cause a coma. They are reported to impair motor skills thus the person taking them should not drive. It is known that individuals who take barbiturates also indulge in alcohol. The next times you sniff a beautiful aroma on some chick's skin remember you are inhaling alcohol. When the hubby finally gets around to doing that paint job you have nagged him to finish for months, the bright colours are laced with alcohol. If your nearest and dearest comes over all starry eyed as romantic darts fling from his moon eyes, think to yourself is this the alcohol in the74perfume or alcohol on his breath, or the alcohol in the freshly painted room. Alcohol depresses the central nervous system; his calm exterior could be dispelling its euphoric effects.

We appear to live in a chemical nightmare unaware of the dangers to ourselves and our loved ones. Alcohol that is the best known destructive fluid to effect the liver, is the black sheep of chemicals, while is shoulders the blame the other drugs of abuse, prescribed drugs and the many pollutants are free to continue their work of building up in the most vital organ alongside the heart.

Remember our body cannot live without a liver.

Prescribed Drugs as an Anaesthetic

Previous captures give us an insight into how the liver plays a vital role in filtering waste and toxins from the body. It controls hormonal balance and helps our immune system to fight infection. We have covered how nutrition is broken down by enzymes(chemical compounds) Needed for the breaking down of protein into amino acids, complex carbohydrates into sugar which in turn is converted into energy, and fat into fatty acids that ensures we have good neurotransmitter connection between synaptic impulses. We know that for good gut bacteria we must eat a daily helping of fresh fruit and vegetables. We have covered the health risks of continuous stress and the problematic results it has on the immune system.

We are aware of the role of vitamins and minerals and there interaction in both body and good mental health

We also saw why Reiki can be successful because is works on the endocrine system especially the fourth chakra where the liver, gallbladder, pancreas lie. Remember the liver, gallbladder, pancreas are responsible for the manufacturing of bile or juices the help with the elimmation of toxic waste from the body by way of stools, sweat vomit and urine. Our adrenal gland also lies within this region and is connected to the energy channels running along the spine. These centres collect energy. Age is reported to be linked to our energy.

Staying young is said to be due to not only to what we eat and drink but to keeping the endocrine system filled with positive energy. Think about it, those monks or holy men who are connected spiritually, mentally, emotionally don't have to use expensive day or night creams. Their chakras are whirling ten to the dozen as they deal only in positive lifestyle their sole purpose is self contentment they have mastered the task of realizing that peace or contentment does not originate in a bottle of brightly contained pills, though the eye of a needle, or weekly visits to a surgery of coughing depressed people who lag behind in the stakes of recognition that we are all in control of our own destiny, and can be as pure as the driven health stakes if we stopped trying to please all around us who want to control the way we love, work, respect, or believe unconditionally that their way is the only way.

Their anxiety, fear, phobias, frustrations, emotional pain appears to have sunk into the earth sprouting beautiful gardens and beds of herbs. In contrast to the everyday Joe who has lines as deep as spud furrows edged along their mouth, eyes, brow or their forehead, could this be the result of a sluggish metabolism. As we know our metabolism is lined to hormones, the thyroid gland plays an important role in this. Hormones are not a foreign entity they are chemicals released into the bloodstream by a gland or tissue.

Our brain, kidneys, intestines all release hormones. Metabolism of cells, growth, and sexual development can be attributed to the function of hormones. One important function is the body's response to stress or illness. Hormones do not live outside our body but are part and parcel us. The old saying of we are what we eat rings as true as the bell that tones every-day to announce that we are a good Christian country. The liver metabolises carbohydrates, proteins and fat by converting glucose and galacteus into glycogen.

By storing this substance it maintains a ready-made storehouse in case of emergency. When our intake of certain carbohydrates is not sufficient, protein and fat are converted to produce insulin to keep sugar levels even. Hormone balance if disturbed can result in water retention, cravings or bloating. Proteins essential for waste management especially bad cholesterol or insulin, it is then eliminated via the kidneys. How do we learn about the human, well we do so because learned men and women wrote about it.

The simple fact is we are told that we must feed out body for optimum health. Most drugs are chemicals substances that alter the function of one or more body organs or change the process of a disease. Drugs include prescribed medicines, over the counter remedies, alcohol, tobacco, and of course those that come under the heading drugs of abuse. Heroin, hash, cocaine, Crack. Tea, coffee, cola drinks, contain caffeine which is both a stimulant drug and a diuretic drug.

Drugs are either prescribed by a doctor, or over the counter each drug has three names, a detailed descriptive chemical name, a shorter generic name that has been approved and a name chosen by the drug company that manufactures it. Formerly drugs were naturally occurring substances extracted from animals, plants, and minerals. Drugs that are manufactured today are manmade, produced artificially in a laboratory setting to ensure potency (strength) that is said to be safer for medical use. Drugs are classified according to their chemical makeup,

Drugs are tested for their efficiency and safety. Tests go through three stages

Laboratory trails.

Animals

Laboratory trails on human beings

And lastly clinical trials on human beings

Whenever the drug companies comply with certain standards they are awarded the department of health licence.

If drugs prove toxic they are withdrawn and the licence withdrawn.

Drugs are used in the treatment, prevention, or diagnosis of a disease, they are prescribed to relive physical or mental symptoms, or to replace a deficient natural substance (like Eltroxin) to replace the hormone in the thyroid. Or crestor to bring down cholesterol,

Drugs are also given to destroy bacteria or viruses As in H. I. V. Vaccines are given to stimulate the body's immune system. Studies show that Antibiotic, painkillers and tranquillizers are among the most commonly prescribed drugs.

Drugs act on the cells of the body by stimulating or blocking chemical reactions,

Tranquiller such as barbiturates are a depressant they depress the central nervous, alcohol, heroin, methadone suppresses the craving for heroin.

These work by binding to a specific receptor site on the cells surface that has a similar structure to the drug. I mentioned in a previous capture how our natural endorphins are similar to heroin and long term use of heroin results in a natural endorphin redundancy. An interesting observation considering that most of those on methadone have problems coming off probably as a result of unfulfilled receptors sites, the main reasons that methadone was introduced was to help those dependent on heroin to detox from the drug . But the medical profession are now aware that methadone is as addictive as the drug it replaced. Drug interaction is common among those using methadone ,most drugs can and do produce harmfully or unpleasant reactions, we see this with methadone ,lack of appetite, constipation ,blotted belly and a liver strung out on toxins. Any change in the absorption, breakdown or elimination of the drug by the liver or kidneys can increase concentration in the blood thus a risk of side effects.

These can be an allergic reaction the formation of antibodies that damage the tissue, a genetic disorder (lack of a specific enzyme that is responsible for activating the drug.

Side effects of drug over load are jaundice, anaphylactic shock.

A drug is useful only when its overall benefits to the patient out weight the risk and severity of any adverse effects. Can this be said of Methadone takers if they cannot stop without withdrawal symptoms as dire as those of heroin?

Prescribed drugs work on receptor sites on the brain they are scientifically produced to resemble molecules units of a substance that has characteristic properties of brain chemicals. Molecules in D N A (deoxyribonucleic acid) consists of thousands of atoms of carbon, hydrogen, oxygen, nitrogen, and phosphorus linked together to form a double-helix spiral structure.

Our body consists of neurons and nerves all different in size and appearance these project from short branches known as dendrites along with the cell body receive impulses from other neurons (a neuron is a specialized cell in any given part of the body) muscles and glands by the axon.

And the swellings at the end called the synaptic terminals. The gap that exists between the terminal and cell body is known as the synaptic gap. The travelling impulse triggers a chemical or neurotransmitter which travels across the gap stimulating the next cell or neuron,

In order for transmitters to work they must be received by receptors. (Specialized cells) We have these throughout our body the central nervous system skin, joints, muscles; these cells can detect chemical changes which become impulses which travel along the sensory neurons.

The brain has motor neurons that carry signals to the muscles and glands, which in turn release chemicals (hormones) unto the body .(Adrenal and cortical for stress)

Information is transmitted along neurons as electrochemical impulses this action potential can occurs because ion channels and pumps are embedded in cell membranes. (protein Molecules).

Neurotransmitters or chemicals bind to neuroreceptors molecules in the receiving cell membrane; they must fit together to either give an excitatory or inhibitory effect.

The action of the neurotransmitter is usually brief ensuring that the chemical is reabsorbed (reup- take) this natural procedure means that the terminal does not have to manufacture more of the same chemical. Other neurotransmitters are broken up by enzymes in the body. These proteins regulate chemical reaction in the body that in turn need a component called a coenzyme and which we get from vitamins and minerals.

The methadone users depression, insomnia, hormone function especially regards to adrenal could therefore result from a change in chemical structure of enzymes or a deficiency in the vitamins and minerals needed to make the healthy coenzymes for proper enzyme function.

Liver enzymes are affected by certain drugs such as barbiturates causing drug interaction if the individual is consuming other medication.

Some methadone users avail of alcohol, bensos, cocaine, medication for hepatitis, or mental problems such as psychosis, or schizophrenia. Allergies and inhalers.

Pharmacists make drugs to influence mental functions and mood these opiates enter the neurotransmitter- receptor and mimic natural chemicals by either blocking out or affect the reuptake of certain neurotransmitters.

Depression is attributed to low serotonin levels this substance is found in tissues and blood platelets, the lining of the digestive tract and the brain. It has many purposes like constricting blood vessels, inhibits gastric secretion. It is important in that it helps with the transmission of nerve impulses between cells.

One of the drugs that manipulate the brain chemicals dopamine and norepinephrine is the drug chlorpromazine and reserpine. Used to treat schizophrenia.

Cocaine and amphetamines work in this way by slowing down the reup-take of the neurotransmitter Norepinephrine activating the neurons for longer periods and causing the effects of more energy, less sleep, aggressiveness.

Lithium which is prescribes to those with bipolar disorder works by speeding up reuptake allowing the individual's mood to become depressed.

Smoking has a similar effect it raises serotonin levels keeping the mood high

One reason that smokers experience a drop in mood whenever they try to quit and why they indulge in an eating binge. (Certain foods raise serotonin levels)

This knowledge has allowed an influx of profits for drug companies to manufacture chemicals to treat symptoms such as anxiety, stress, lack of coping skills, emotional problems that could perhaps be better served with an overall of the persons diet, vitamin and mineral count or a visit to a counsellor where they can discuss the matter in private away from a society built on right or wrong and judgment.

Sweetness and Contentment

What is a toxin? It is a harmful substance that affects the proper functioning of the body. Each day this army of toxins or chemicals invade the body sending the liver into overdrive as it struggles to deal with the onslaught. If as mentioned in the previous pages we suffer a sluggish liver, the remaining organs are affected in some way. The toxins overload prevents the liver from processing or breakdown the deadly substances, like rabbits fleeing a burrow, they head for the bloodstream where the immune system believes it is under attack so it must act. If someone on methadone is consuming the equivalent of 2,960 mills a month, drinks alcohol. is on Interferon for an already damaged liver due to hepatitis, takes antidepressants, sleeping pills, how can the liver regenerate itself it is under consent attack from a barrage of toxins . Like an overslept monk it must work consistently to rid itself of the onslaught to survive and remain in a healthy balance. Everyone knows that this resilient organ unlike the brain cells replenishes itself, but only if the abuser of alcohol stops his drinking. If the methadone liver does not get space to breath what will the ongoing damage be? A toxic liver is a sluggish liver one intent on damaging both the immune system and the brain. A weak immune system means more infection, flu, or viris, Methadone is cost effective, and it costs less to sustain someone on the green diesel due to its longevity in comparison to heroin. What effect does this sugary syrup have on the liver long-term? Sugar is reported to interfere with the absorption of protein. It can cause food allergies, anddiabetes. It can increase the size of the liver by making the liver cells divide, can cause damage to the pancreas, increase retention of fluid, can cause headaches. It is reported to cause an increase in Delta Alpha and the brain waves. Sugar lowers the enzymes ability to function and we have already read how these enzymes are so important in the human body. It can cure skin ageing by changing the structure of collagen. It is said to contribute to high cholesterol, osteoporosis, and varicose veins. In children it is reported that those with eczema have a high intake of sugar. Blood pressure rises if sugar intake is high. Can cause bad bowel movement. This is evident in methadone users, constipation is a common complaint. Depression can be a result of too much sugar. It is associated with kidney stones. One frightening effect is its ability to increase acid in stools and bacterial enzymes in the colon. This can result in cancer causing compounds and colon cancer.

It can cause oxidative stress; cancer loves it because it feeds it. When we consume large amounts of sugar the livers ability to break down fat is reduced due to bad functioning of 77proteins, albumin and lipoprotein.

Gallbladder cancer according to some sources is attributed to sugar. It can also affect the adrenal glands, releasing the hormone responsible for aggression it does so by way of slowing down functioning as we read in earlier chapters. This gland is important for the release of adrenal, the hormone adrenalin in time of fear, anxiety. Irritable bowel is a disease attributed to over consumption of sugar. Most important it can cause liver tumours. Aspartame which is an artificial sweetener consumed by millions is another hidden sugar danger.

Felicity Lawrence who writes for the Guardian (15 July 2005) in her article. She states that concern was expressed by the European Food Safety Authority, who considered the matter high priority. The is artificial sweetener is used in more than 6,000 food and drink products. Researchers in Italy at the Institute of Cancer Research reported that tests on animals especially females Aspartame caused lymphomas and leukaemia. The doses given to these animals corresponded to the daily intake of humans. Some individual suffered convulsions following the ingestion of soft drinks sweetened by Aspartame. Diabetes which affects 17 million people in America. The consumption of sugar sweetened beverages has increased according to Mein Stampfer of the Harvard School of Public Health in Boston.

Sarah Boseley (21 April 2003) reported how the sugar industry in America threatened to bring the World Health Organisation to its knees by demanding that congress end its funding to(WHO scraps guidelines on healthy eating). The Sugar Association said it would challenge the report by WHO to stop the $260 million funding. Next time you dig your spoon into the dainty flowered bowl filled with white sugar, think of how it arrives at your table. Beets of sugarcane are crushed; this releases juice which is then boiled into syrup. Processing the syrup into white graduals is done by filtering through a channel or chemical resin filter. By granulating or milking grains we get sugar. Sugar comes under the name molasses, confectioners' sugar, and brown sugar. Brown sugar, corn syrup, table sugar, sucrose are refined sweeteners. The function of the immune system is to fight invading bacteria. Sugar, honey can interfere with the ability of white blood cells to destroy bacteria. Sugar is used as a food additive in most processed foods as we saw in the previous chapters. The immune system is damaged in HIV. Methadone is laced with sugar, so it can only add to an already workload of the immune system and liver. It also causes teeth decay. May of that on methadone have little or no teeth?

Killing me Softly

Dentures are a common occurrence in young people who have not yet reached thirty. Methadone is sweetened with sugar or sweeteners. Those who make or distribute this Opoid must make every effort to ensure that the upmost precaution is attended to in order to reduce the side effects of the hidden dangers to those receiving green diesel. Liver, teeth, bones, Hepatitis C or B all of these are affected by over exposure to toxic substances.

Food additives are another source of toxin. These are found in shelf life foods, people buying weekly shop can look at the labels, the tin, and bottle, can in order to eliminate the danger of pumping extra chemicals, sugar, salt or sodium into an already overloaded liver. Saccharin -an artificial sweetener believed to cause tumours in test animals. Aspartame; Low calorie sugar is reported to cause skin hives and swelling of throat tissues (Science News June 1986). Sensitivity to monosodium glutamate causes headaches, flushing and intestinal upset. I myself have an allergy to this product. On consuming it in food I get violently ill and faint. Children's cereals like Frosted Flakes scientists who study nutrition have found that while less sugar is in the ingredients the manufacturers replaced sugar with refined carbohydrates so the crunch is still there.

Addictive treatment centres do usually follow best medical practice in the management and care of those receiving methadone. But like any practice this depends on the individual doctor and his expertise and knowledge around the individual's health. Doctors are human and are only as knowledgeable as their patient's information. As reported in earlier chapters all medications are metabolised via the liver. Blood levels can be affected by liver disease. Methadone and luiprenorphone can interact with pharmacological properties similar to morphine its clearance from the body is important if drug accumulation is to be avoided. Its life span is 24hours to heroin's 3-4 hours making it cost efficient to the cost of keeping someone on heroin. It stops carvings, but not everyone ingesting this green diesel is in good health, someone with ceoliac disease and who has poor absorption, which is pregnant, who is dual drugging on Valium, antidepressants, cocaine, alcohol, diet, Hepatitis B or C. Research has indicated that liver toxicity is not present in individuals on methadone. But methadone does cause weight gain in most individuals consuming it. Weight gain is due to the livers inability to break down fat. It cannot do so due to an overload of chemicals or toxins in the body. As mentioned previously bile needs to be secreted in order for it to carry out the much needed task of elimination.

When the liver fails to neutralise toxins by way of using enzymes to break chemical bonds holding the toxins, the substances become non-toxic and are excreted as urine, sweat, faeces, breath, and mucus. The lungs, kidneys, skin and intestines should all work in unison for the body to stay healthy. If the liver is not functioning as it should it can become overworked by the continuous supply of toxins allowing these to get into the bloodstream which results in weight gain, bloating, mood swings, depression. It is this weight gain that I have noticed most in women taking methadone.

It gathers around the abdomen like an inflated tyre. This then must be taken as an indication of a sick liver. Sick to death of high doses of thin green diesel dumped into young bodies in an effort at containing crime, managing lives in communicates that suffer mental burnout before the age of thirty five. Evidence shows that methadone overdose is on the increase. (Maxwell 2005) carried out a study in Texas reported in his findings that over 20% of patients in methadone treatment suffered death due to liver disease, 18% died of heart attack, while 14% died of drug overdose.

From working in methadone treatment, I have found that duel drugging is common. Individuals indulge in cocaine, hash, Valium, sleeping pills and alcohol. The green diesel may keep them homeostasis and stop cravings but it does not give the much needed high that most need. The social problems, emotional problems, fears, insecurity, low self-esteem are only eliminated when they attend counselling. Self-esteem rises when education is given. Confidence building, drama therapy, art all play a role in their much needed expression to be accepted, loved, respected, liked, cared for. Independence is crucial for the methadone dependant individual to move forward. Duel drugging is the big thing in a lot of individuals receiving the green diesel by mixing this lethal cocktail the abuse can reinvent the high he or she first received when taking heroin.

Cocaine is the favourite among methadone users. This illicit drug presents its abuser with a confidence boost. His feeling of importance increases, he becomes hyper, can solve any problem. Hash, grass, prescribed drugs all used by some individuals who are using the thick green substitute for heroin. Alcohol is also abused especially at weekends as part time hip- hops into the underprivileged estates, house parties, children's parties, birthdays, granny's anniversary, and the dog's new pups. It can be any excuse to indulge in chilling out that much needed drug to wipe out tomorrow.

When this green god is mixed with alcohol or prescription drugs such as antidepressants, sedatives, uppers, stimulants or other black market drugs the consequences can be an overdose. In New Mexico evidence suggests that in (1998-2002) 50.3% deaths occurred from mixing methadone and illicit drugs. If for example the individual is taking drugs for depression they need to inform their doctor otherwise the combination can be dangerous.

Buprenophine is now almost avoided in patients suffering from liver disease, Interferon: a drug used to treat the liver, especially individuals suffering from Hepatitis is known to have many side effects one of which is heart failure.

The American Journal of Medicine carried out a community based evaluation of sudden death associated with therapeutic levels of methadone. This group of doctors studied those receiving methadone over a period of four years. Their study showed that a total of 22 sudden cardiac deaths occurred in these centres 23%. It was concluded that cardiac disease in the case group even at therapeutic levels are a likely cause of sudden death. They make the recommendation that chemical safeguards and further studies needed to be undertaken as a means of safety in methadone treatment.

This synthetic opiate has a long life span in comparison to heroin. It has rapid muscle absorption. It is legal and on the increase due to its low cost. It is an economical alternative to more expensive opiates. While reports show that green diesel can be responsible for cardiac arrest, which is attributed to the blockage of potassium ion channels. This prolongation of cardiac arrest with a prolonged interval on the electrocardiogram.

Molly or green diesel is community based. Clinics are set up usually on the periphery of those communities most devastated by heroin abuse. Doctors specialize and have to register and comply in a medical setting. The communities most affected are also the most under educated, underprivileged in society living off social welfare with little means of conducting any studies, on an opiate that is more addictive than the one they are trying to detox from. Both respiratory depression and some cardiac arrhythmias. Some individuals who suffer from asthma are also taking methadone. The study was a well defined one carried out and evaluated by the medical examiner. Post mortem was conducted. A total of 72 patients with evidence of toxicological tests carried out. The person's medical history is all important when methadone is prescribed. Stomach proteins (colitis), low mineral levels (potassium), Magnesium (heart disease), allergies, alcohol add to dizziness and drowsiness. Drug interaction - all prescriptive over counter drugs, psychiatric drugs, desipramine, tranquilliser, sleep medication Drugs that affect certain liver enzymes (the herb of John Wort), antibiotics, anti-seizure medications,, laxatives (methadone causes constipation).

Reuters Health reports that a number of cases of unexplained death from sudden cardiac death can be blamed on taking regular therapeutic doses of methadone.

Cocktail of Chemicals

The immune system is of special importance to me as my work deals with individuals who have HIV or hepatitis. This defence mechanism needs to be kept well oiled to function properly. When an invading bacteria, attacks the body the immune system goes into overdrive, the thymus gland plays an important role by producing hormones to stimulate white blood cells. It is these cells that are the body's first line of defence. When we are stressed or have a catalogue of emotional problem, the thymus can become overworked. By performing Reiki across the area beneath the throat and heart or placing a turquoise at the nape of your neck you can enhance the life force energy. Turquoise is a wonderful colour to wear if you feel stressed as it calms the nerves; it provides you with courage and puts a shield of protection around your area from destructive negative thinking like anger, envy. This stress buster also helps with your relaxing process, allowing you to breath into your belly and not short breaths that are associated with stress. By situating a number of turquoise crystals about your body while relaxing you can strengthen your immune system this practice is especially good for HIV sufferers or those having treatment for hepatitis.

Lie down in a warm place. Place four crystals at each side of you. Then place one below your feet and at the crown of your head, place your hands on the area of your chest between the throat and heart, remember don't cross your hands, close all fingers. You can stay like this until you feel the need to remove them, which can be anything from ten to twenty minutes. This shall strengthen your immune system, allowing it to fight infection. It is not however a cure, you shall need to continue to be under your doctor's supervision. It does however eliminate stress that impacts and weakens the immune system. Pain is associated with concentrated energy that needs to be balanced.

The pharmaceutical companies have made a fortune on the back of pain, but taking medicine for pain that is controllable can add to the imbalance causing more problems than it solves. The holistic way of using crystals to relieve pain is simple and non-toxic. Smokey quartz is a good leveller for pain and helping to fight addiction. Once the concentrated energy is released you can complement the healing process with clear quartz. Arthritis can be helped by holding a smoky quartz over the area affected with pain.

Tissue can be repaired by placing a quartz crystal on each side of the body. If you are one of those parents who have a hyperactive child and you don't know where to escape to, to have some space you can try this exercise with lapis. Lapis this beautiful dark stone can help both you and your child to receive the much needed rest you require. This stone balances the third eye and throat chakra, it releases points of view that border on destruction, and it helps the receiver to have clarity and to listen. Then sit back as your child sits without disruption for a few god given seconds. You can also place this in a safe place somewhere in your child's room so they can have a peaceful sleep.

If you have the misfortune to be in a relationship where one partner is possessive, perhaps you are on a programme or you have started your journey of self development, because that journey was disrupted by your need for abusive substances at a tender age, you gave your power away to those who continually informed you of the shame you brought on your family, or perhaps your marriage disintegrated due to your drugging habit. So now you have taken the path of recovery, you have entered a methadone treatment programme, so you are accepted by all and sundry. But those closest to you may have been hurt by your spiral of abuse, trust, respect have been destroyed. This needs to be replenished, so you comply by returning to the fold. You are forever grateful to sleep with a roof over your head, to be fed, feel wanted, accepted, liked, to belong to family again.

This catch twenty-two has a twist. You have the privilege of personal development, counselling, education that opens your horizons. You are moving forward emotionally, psychologically. You are ahead of the posse. Your partner, family are not. They still love but are judgemental, that is what they know, society's restrictions. Some people call them the (begrudges), but it is fear. You are in an environment where you learn that loving yourself is empowering, that unconditional love releases you from shame, guilt, sadness, loneliness. Your have found balance, you are content.

The people in your life were not strung out on dope, did not experience the highs of heroin, the lows of withdrawal, did not snort cocaine and believe they could do the job of Brian Cowen. They have nothing to feel shame or guild about. They have forgiven you, taken you back into the fold, accepted you within the community just as long as your treatment programme is situated on the periphery of their housing estate hidden from their front door so the nosy neighbours can't see you come and go. Thus becoming aware that you are receiving opium to replace opium, allowing you a sense of being normal.

Anyway they are human and can't afford to see drop in house prices. So when they don't want you to change, tell you are behaving in an unreasonable way, to drop the self pity or attitude, that the centre is doing your head in , you could hand them a pink sapphire crystal to help their feeling of possessiveness, which is a result of imbalance, manipulated love experienced during childhood.

Their paranoia or jealousy is attributed to their need to control when you are drugging. You needed them, you depended on their support. Now you are learning to become independent and you want equality in your relationship this new-found freedom can sometimes place a spanner in the dependent works as they see their control slipping away like a slim ball falling from a secure place. The guilt game may come into full flow remember it is used against the heroin user to keep them in place. Whenever this occurs place a crystal of halite in your pocket or better still present it to those trying to return to old out worn conditioning as a gesture of love, informing them of how it allows them to let go of negative emotions.

Guilt can be released by Halite; you can stop being the scapegoat by carrying this stone. Emotional blackmail is part of control. You can dispel these negative emotions of not being wanted as a child, receiving the blunt of physical or verbal abuse over others in the family. You feel unloved, believed you should never have been born. Guilt leaves you feeling unfulfilled, you may become a people pleaser, a perfectionist, noting is right, and you blame yourself for everything that goes wrong in your personal life. This beautiful sodium chloride comes in colours of blue, pink yellow. Blue halite helps you love yourself, to forgive as the higher source has done years ago. It shall draw out negative energies especially around drugs.

I use crystals for my Reiki healing. This chakra therapy is a wonderful tool in cleaning negative energy from the charkas. I use this method as well as counselling as a means of speeding up the release of stagnated emotional issues.

Crystal therapy is a good helper; the beautiful coloured stones focus the mind, give peace and a sense of self. I use certain stones to clear my working space of negative energy. All holistic therapies complement each other as they work on the energy field and are chemical free. No
Synthetic substance is invading the body.

In the following chapters I shall deal with and encounter the pitfalls of processed foods. How these foods build up in the liver. By keeping an open mind on all aspects of healing both medically and holistically we can offer the most effective service to those who would best benefit from it. Green diesel does stabilise the individual in that it is prescribed legally the daily grind of having to steal from all around is diminished allowing the individual to help the government keep down crime. Green diesel is deceptive in that it gives a false sense to the user. Like a Machiavellian mask its appearances are truthful, honest, given with good intentions, makes money for its, makers and dispensers .its hidden dangers are concealed as craftily as the rattle snake waiting in the deep grass. It is not all that it is supposed to be, simple because it is still in the experimental stage, like the child learning to walk.

This cost effective opiod helps in that it opens the opportunity to get much help needed help for those who have run the gauntlet of the up and downs of feeding a heroin habit. It is a life-line in a no win situation, a stop gap in the torment of hopelessness, feelings of failure and exclusion from a society built on conditional love. A love curled around rules and regulations.

By opening the throat chakra the suppressed feelings are released allowing the individual to talk freely with a counsellor.

Doctors who work at these centres can give their clients the choice to choose what treatment best suits them. An overview of all aspects of health needs to be considered if their overall health is to be improved. Diet, allergies, pollutants, hormone induced meat; farmed salmon are known to have a lighter shade of pink to their fresh water counterpart.

Natural Killers

The immune system fights against bacteria and viruses. This collection of cells and proteins protect the body from harmful micro organisms. The digestive tract breaks down the food we eat. When some of our food escapes into the blood stream allergies result. White cells are the gladiators of the immune system they pump out their cell chest dividing into several cells. By secreting antibodies they lock themselves into the invading bacteria giving them a run for their money. This procedure stops the invading bacteria's stopping them from producing toxins, viruses cannot reproduces when they are stopped from gaining control of the cell.

T cells have intelligence second to none; they are produced at the thymus gland, which lies between the heart and throat. We saw in the last chapter how a turquoise crystal or Reiki can help to clear emotional blockages that accumulate at the throat, the person who has difficulty communicating their feelings or fears to those around them, be it for emotional or other reasons that lead to stress shall be the first to experience a weakened thymus gland. Leaving them prone to infections and flu like symptoms. Someone who is always catching colds would do well to examine their reaction to certain emotional issues. If the symptoms persist a look at diet, plus a visit to their G.P should not be ignored.

Some foods such as gluten which has a protein found in wheat that damages the lining of the small intestine due to hypersensitivity. This protein is also found in rye, cereals.

Gliadin is wheat protein.

Hording belongs to the barley family.

Secalin belongs to its cousin Rye.

Aveniis found in oat one of my favourite breakfasts and one I'd die for, but am unable to consume due to my coeliac intolerance. If an individual has an allergy to gluten they must watch that their died does not include bread made from the above mentioned. Also of the list is white or brown, cakes, biscuits, baking powder, take communion, frozen chips, bistro, white flour, cheese spreads, soy sauce, dry roasted nuts, food from fast outlets, fish fried in batter ,this is a double whammy as it is flour and deep fried.

Shelf life foods also contain a host of hidden gluten. Mustard powder is another offender and gluten holder. All processed meats, ham, crisps, should be avoided at all costs these delicious demons are laced with the proverbial lashings of salt that mineral that can send blood scoring through the roof and is fried in trans fats to boot.

Some fizzy drinks not only contain barley four but are laced with that hidden danger sugar.

Most sweets, some tablets are coated or filler, also alcoholic beverages.

Coffee that comes from any vending machine, barley water, Guinness our best export , stout, beer all contain grain.

Food intolerance can cause weight gain. Excess fluid in the tissues sets off a chain reaction within the body. The immune system attacks the foreign invader, histamine and chemicals are released into the bloodstream as the immune system goes into full flight in its effort at protecting the embattled cells. To complicate matters endorphins, the natural opiates flood the body. These hormones provide a feeling that the world is rosy which lasts momentarily before the body goes into freefall seeking a fix of the food that started the reaction in the first place. Hormones are secreted from the adrenal glands and the individual gets a boost of energy, mood lifts, blood sugar is lowered, insulin is destabilised,

Carbohydrates are a must as cells are starved of energy which is provided by the pancreas (remember the pancreas is connected to the chakra). The immune system acts as a gladiator, its function to ensure that noting enters the cells when bacteria attack the body. It homes in like a drunk seeking a last drink before closing. Bacteria need to multiply as devious as the husband when he wants a night out with the lads. It waits its chance hanging our waiting for the right moment to pounce. It is now known that bacteria has in intellect all of its own. It can send information to cousin bacteria about the makeup of antibiotics. This improved in our hospitals today, with the growing rise of M.R.S A that crafty infectious disease that lurks under dirty finger nails or the hands of the lazy nurse of medical person who refuse to a hear to the regulations and welfare to their charges.

If the battered body is not down and out by the sensitivity to gluten, it must then undergo a thrashing of neurotransmitters as they reduce serotonin, that much needed hunger controller, and mood balancer. When serotonin is reduced and can't send the much needed information that your belly is full and you should sell tape your mouth, you are convinced that you haven't placed a morsel of grub pass your glossy lipstick and head for the fridge to gorge yourself on more high carbohydrates, that shall land around your once small waist sending you into the pit of diet despair.

The malfunctioning of the thyroid gland that fat burner of the body. When it is either overactive or underactive you are faced with a choice, overactive you may never have to pass a chocolate factory again because you shall be unable to maintain weight, underactive you shall only have to glance sideways at a cream bun and the pounds shall pile on. The important hormone production is what sends signals to the other body parts so that these can be interpreted correctly.

Large food manufacturers use the protein gluten in a lot of their products as well as that other body destroyer sugar. Cereal, couscous, fillers, flour, porridge oats, rolled oats, children's rusks,semolina, wheat- germ, wheat- starch,, thickened malt, oat bran, vegetable starch the list goes on and on. If you are a male do not despair, you definitely can't lean your foot on the counter railing and sip the top from the black stuff (Guinness) but you can compensate by going posh with a glass of champagne, wine, whiskey, spirits, sherry. Forget the pint glass if you are intolerant to gluten, or you shall have to make a dash for the nearest loo with a dose of the (trots), I don't mean the soap on T.V., diarrhoea, thyroid problems, weight loss (I like that one), diabetes, a bloated belly so you have to unbutton your belt every time you eat your dinner, mouth ulcers, vomiting, tiredness. I remember before I was diagnosed with coeliac disease I would start hovering the house in the morning only to take many breaks before finishing around noon having to have constant lay downs due to chronic tiredness. Even today I attend one of the best men dealing in this area who can looks at my insides with an instrument every six months to ensure I am in good working order. Mind you I do have to fork out a set sum of money for the privilege, but as they say "I am worth it"

When someone suffers from this disease, the villi which help with food absorption are destroyed by the immune system (like a giant plant swallowing flies that land near it). The flat villi then loses its ability to do its given task of helping nutrients absorption, malabsorption occurs and some nutrients are passed straight out of the body. As we saw it is these nutrients that are needed to maintain healthy cells. Like methadone, coeliac disease can result in osteoporosis or thinning of the bone marrow, so if someone is a coeliac and is on high maintenance of methadone they may be twice at risk of this loss of bone mass. There are of course lots of healthy foods a coeliac can enjoy and I personally don't have a problem sticking to a gluten diet. At the end of the book I have included some healthy recipes. Some shall help you to combat over toxicity of the liver from both prescribed drugs and methadone. I have also shown how you can have intolerance to a substance or food and not have to feel like an alien. Herbs, exercises are all inclusive of a happy healthy body. It's not all doom and gloom but it is important for those taking methadone to enhance good eating habits by ensuring a proper intake of vitamins and minerals, which can be disrupted if they have an allergy to gluten, pollon, dust, and smoking peanuts. Absorption is the name of the game, if we are not receiving this from the food we ingest then we can hardly expect to remain in a healthy state.

Laying in Weight

Weight gain is the one thing I noticed in dealing with individuals receiving methadone. I would see a young man or woman start the programme only to witness massive weight gain in a matter of months. There are a number of ways we put on weight that is weight gain occurs if our eating is out of balance. Because our weight remains more or less stable if dietary energy matches energy expenditure. I needed to examine what was causing the once slim beautiful young person on methadone

Who expanded life a balloon filled with helium gas? Energy is what keeps the body functioning. It consists of billions of cells which need nutrients for cell renewal and energy to mobile muscles, brain, nerves, and hormones. We are like a giant electrical powerhouse. We take in nutrients by way of food, carbohydrate proteins, fats, minerals, vitamins. A good diet supplies adequate but not excessive quantities of protein, carbohydrates, fats, minerals, vitamins, fibre and water, so our daily diet should include food from the four main sources, milk and milk products such as cheese, breads, cereals, meat, eggs, pulses, the vitamins or minerals we should get from the food we eat.

If however someone has an illness coeliac disease vitamins or minerals can be administered due to mal-absorption. If we consume only carbohydrates and not enough protein our body would suffer a deficiency or excess of a certain nutrient. The presence of a poisonous element or toxin can also disrupt our metabolism. If we eat too much protein and not enough carbohydrates we suffer because of the imbalance. In Africa we often see how poverty caused malnutrition due to this imbalance. (Anorexia Nervosa) when individuals restrict their diet they suffer from deficiencies.

Those who depend on drugs or alcohol can lose interest in food, grabbing chips or burgers as a quick fix to a hectic life style thus their health and liver can suffer because of bad eating habits. Deficiency of specific nutrients (foods) is associated with Crone's disease and also coeliac disease when the person is allergic to gluten found in most breads and everything associated with four or wheat.

Obesity or weight gain results from a number of things but mostly when we can't stay away from robbing the cupboard or fridge and as a result we gorge ourselves with food that saturate our bodies with almost everything we consume in the supermarket shelves has suger,salt, colouring

105

,chemicals to give it a long life span . Fat then can become the new rage; it has a nasty habit of crawling up on you un-noticed. The more fat or refined carbohydrates we scoff into our dainty mouths, the more we need to fill the ever widening gap.

As more and more junk food is ingested following binging sessions especially at the weekends.

Fats and oil fats are lipids. Fats consist of fatty acids divided into saturated and unsaturated, depending on the proportion of hydrogen atoms. Whenever the fatty acids contain the highest quantity of hydrogen it is saturated fat. Polyunsaturated fat, we also get fat from meat, dairy products are saturated fat. Vegetable fats these are in certain oils for frying or chips are unsaturated. The amount of fat in our diet can influence our health. Essential fatty acids can be found in vitamins A, D and E. Our body stores fat as energy reserves in times of illness. Steroids or cholesterol are found in animal and plant tissue which are converted into hormones or vitamins. Bile salt emulsified dietary fats before they are broken down by enzymes in the pancreas. The lymphatic system or lymph nodes are found under the armpit, in the groin or at the neck. Once broken down the fats are carried by the lymphatic system they enter the bloodstream (HDLS) pick up cholesterol carrying it back to the liver where it is processed and excreted by the kidneys. The liver also processes end products, chemical substances. It helps clear the blood of drugs and toxins by breaking them down for excretion by the bile. The liver needs to be kept in good condition if it is to function properly. All drugs, pollutants, toxins, chemicals are detoxified by the liver. The daily intake of methadone if it be 80 ml or 120 ml must be broken down for your body to remain in a healthy condition. The bile that is secreted from the gallbladder joins forces with the liver to maintain a build up of toxins does not occur. Nutrients or the food we put into our bodies each day helps to make up the bile salts essential for the toxin discharge.

Drugs of all descriptions are responsible for the build up of toxins causing depression, confusion, tiredness, sleeplessness. Confusion lessons you chances of coping, of problem solving, of concentration. Toxicity comes from alcohol, heroin, methadone, barbiturates, secondly, zenax, glue, paint, thinner, Valium, codeine, cough mixture, hashish, LSD, cocaine, amphetamines, benso, deadline, caffeine pesticides such as organophosphates used in Britain and Northern Ireland with over a horrendous amount used each year. These are toxic, affecting the central nervous system, they can cause cancer, are linked to defects in the unborn foetus, can interfere with the brains neurotransmitters, hormones. On the physical side they are reported to cause allergies such as asthma, eczema a skin complaint, irritable bowel. I live in the country and have known firsthand the effects that some of these can have on the eyes when spraying begins. The eyes run, and itch the snots flow from your nose and you cough and wheeze like an old person with a chest complaint. I once used commercial flee killer on my cat, then watched in shock as it went into a mad fit of racing around like a have cocked mad thing, like something out of Silence of the Lambs, foaming at the mouth.

I now made up my own flee killer with Tee Tree Oil. The regulations regarding pesticides are not stringent enough when it comes to human health. Like methadone distribution it is deemed cost efficient. It appears that profit is more prized than human life. The next time you are about to punch a forkful of lettuce into your mouth, remember that its dainty green leaves have been doused with a number of chemicals so you can perceive it as appealing, fresh, crisp and so inviting. Residues of dangerous chemicals in the jade green broccoli, Brussels sprouts, celery, the vibrant red strawberries waiting patiently for the dollop of fresh cream to drop upon its head, has been rinsed in chemicals that have travelled long journeys to wet out taste buds. This vegetable exchange could cost your liver a double dose of trouble to have to cope with a cocktail of chemicals that could kill a horse.

Apples, pears, plums, grapes, oranges, peaches can all be immigrants coming from countries that have little regard for chemical input.

Obesity or weight gain results from a number of things mostly from eating more than our body needs. Junk food is an example, the large Mac with fries that have been fired in Trans Fats shall pile weight on all the hips, rear-end, midriff, oils heated at certain temperatures especially saturated oils release chemicals that are bad for our health. High cholesterol, certain cancers are now believed to be linked to a diet high in Tran's fats. When we gorge ourselves on fast food we are depriving our cells of the vitamins and minerals needed to regenerate them. The quick fix food may stop the hunger pangs in our belly but it shall do nothing to counteract the depletion of natural minerals and vitamins missing from a healthy diet rich in greens, beans, fish, which all contain essential fatty acids to fuel your brain. These can be found in flaxseed, hemp, walnut, and pumpkin. A hand- full of these once a day as a snack, mixed with stews, or soups can do wonders for your mind, these can come in, supplement form so your diet is sufficient in omega3 and omega 6. Of course this should always be run by your doctor so as not to interact with any medication you may be taking. Remember balance is the secret to good brain power. By cutting out most processed foods that are stacked with sugar, salt, and preservatives, you shall dispel that bulky middle that sticks to your belly and wrist like a lost soul unable to find its way home. Our brain needs fat it is made up of 60% fat this is not the fat from the deep fryer, which shall clog your arteries, raise your cholesterol levels, or place a Michelin tyre around your midriff, deplete your serotonin that much needed neurotransmitter (chemical) that helps your mood and enables you to deal with emotion, controls appetite, helps keep depression at bay. The next time you are tempted to stand in a line of people with the waft of frying oil drifting beneath your nose, as the alcohol takes effect telling your brain you need a fix of greasy fish stop and think, it shall fill your gut giving you a surge of serotonin reaching your brain but the consequences lead to a mood as fowl as a cockroach searching for mites beneath a bundle of rotten leaves the next day.

That pain in your chest could be a rise in your cholesterol levels from years of consuming fast food.

By setting yourself a healthy eating plan and investing in your health you may be around to play and enjoy your grandchildren. Saturated and monounsaturated fats or hard fats should also be taken in moderation, it is your choice what and how you eat and what you feed to your children.

Think of your body as an expensive car, would you put diesel in a petrol engine. That is what you may be doing to your body every time you eat foods that *are* high *in sugar,* salt, pesticides, if you did not take proper care of your car it would fall apart and the engine would seize, the same applies to your body you and you alone are responsible for its welfare.

Next time you are in a downer ask yourself what you ate

Mr and Mrs Omega

It has now become common knowledge that for our brains to remain healthy and remain in good working order we must feed them the correct vitamins and minerals, so it is important to ensure that as parents we feed our children the correct nutrition that can help them to remain active mentally especially at exam time.

Studies suggest that vitamin C can increase our 1Q. folic acid a member of the important B Vitamins is attributed with helping to up the ante on the intelligence stakes. We first have to look at how neurotransmitters work and why fat is essential if we are to enjoy good mental health. Evidence shows that when we have low intake of essential fats it can affect not only our intelligence but also our memory. As children we are fed with our mother's breast milk because it is made of natural essential fat. Hence the reason why those in the medical profession are keen that each newborn child have the best possible start in life by breast feeding.

A majority of those on Methadone are prone to poor memory, eczema, dry hair, brittle bones, constipation, heart burn, insomnia, hot flushes, sweating, fatigue Our body when starved of the fats it needs, is unable to maintain its natural homeostatic balance, we see this with methadone takers they suffer with phobias, wounds that take long periods to heal, obsessive behaviour, have difficulty concentrating. All linked to a lack of the correct essential fats in their diet. Most of those on methadone may have little or no recourse to family, proper eating, home life or nutritional information from their doctor; therefore continue to feed their bodies on food that is doing them more harm than good. Most previous heroin users would have grown up in the fast food era where their daily intake was chips and buggers a high concentration of refined carbohydrates. The more fast foods we eat the more we needed to regulate serotonin levels.

Many methadone users are deficient in the good fats needed to function in everyday life. Firstly they don't make good food choices, their lifestyle of drugging has robbed them of the responsible of learning to grow, mature, develop life skills, or robbed them of access to education.

By the time they reach a methadone program and see a doctor a lot of damage has already begun, in vitamin and mineral deficiency some suffer with Hepatitis or HIV The doctor's training is the prescribing of drugs legalised ones, a good doctor shall look at the options and alternative to drugs in his or her effort at alleviating anxiety or stress rather than give an antidepressant which only adds to an ail ready toxic state.

So let's look at the omega twins this group of fatty acids which are vital for many body functions, nerves, immune system, and fat transport. These cannot be made by the body therefore we have to get them through our diet. These include eating fish, such as sardines, mackerel, trout, salmon, rapeseed oil. They also help brain development in unborn children, They are equally important as they make up the myelin which is a fatty material made of lipid fat and protein and forms a protective sheath around some nerve fibres and increases the efficiency of nerve impulse transmission.

From blinking our eyes to playing football our body needs the input of neurons, neurotransmitters, endocrine glands, sense organs, spine, are all interactive. Our nervous system allows us to be aware of muscles; glands enable us to adjust to our environment. Our perception of events depends on how the sense organs detect stimuli and how our brain interprets it. Our behaviour is motivated by hunger, thirst, and the avoidance of pain. That we use and understand language or solve everyday problems is down to the complexity of the brain. This body of chemicals, linkages biological processes that is the brain.

Like a gigantic computer it stores, memorises, and recalls the information of everyday experiences.

A mass of neurons, circuits, specialised cells, chemicals, receptors, gaild cells (glue) that holds everything together, all combined to work like clockwork if we feed it the proper nutrition. When we examine the workings of the electrochemical impulse which are like a doughnut that form pores across the cell membrane. These protein structures regulate the flow of electrically charged ions like sodium, potassium, calcium, by opening their pores. The speed at which these impulses travel depends on the myelin sheath which is specialized cells called glial.

Our brain makes prostaglandins (a form of fatty acids) and these acts in a similar way to hormones, these important fats protect our stomach, and duodenum against ulceration, it lowers blood pressure and stimulates contractions in labour.

Amino acids are important in those taking methadone, years of abuse can deplete the natural neurotransmitters such as adrenaline the body's natural morphine supply, and noradrenalin and serotonin all play a role in mood disorder these are in the area of the brain that regulates emotions.

Research shows that depression is associated with a deficiency of one or both of these important neurotransmitters, while mania is caused by an excess. The drug Reserpine that helps to control raised blood pressure can cause depression as it is reported to deplete both serotonin and nor-epinephrine. Some drugs used to treat depression are reported to increase serotonin and nor-epinephrine in the nervous system. While some drugs work as inhibitors that is they block the activity of the enzyme(a protein that regulates the rate of a chemical reaction in the body) by inhibiting the brains natural chemical from reuptake Methadone users are prone to depression and are handed antidepressants as a cure for all, perhaps we need to examine that their sensitivity to depresses mood can be the result of a lack of life skills, no employment, little education, and dependency on others and a lack of social support, a shortage of money to buy the proper nutrition that would provide them with the essential fats needed to feed their brain and nervous system.

Could it be that the medical profession would be out of a job if we had a healthy?
Community

Crystals

Stones and rocks have played a part in many religions ,we see this with Jesus when he said Said to Peter whose name itself means rock, "upon this rock you shall build my church". Moses is also reported to have received the ten commandants on rock, as did the leader of Islam Mohammed, it is said the stones spoke to him. Mecca is a place of pilgrimage; its main focus is the large black stone where every Muslim is expected to visit at least once. Stones are also used for prophesy by many cultures as far back as Alexander the great.

St. Patrick Mountain is considered a holy place of spiritual healing with thousands of people

Visiting it yearly.

Tibetans, Japanese, Chinese, Indians all consider mountains and stones sacred.

In Ireland stones are engraved with symbols as are head stones.

Carved and polished stones are revered in certain parts of the modern world especially gems. The Himalayas is reported to lead to the magical city of Shambhala when reached one could receive eternal youth. Crystals are said to hold beings of light, and are used in a variety of ways from cleaning water to spiritual renewal. I have found in my work with addiction that spirituality is trampled down in despair, like a stagnated pond the methadone taker's energy is blocked. Stones and crystals come from the earth they are used for many forms of healing, the mineral kingdom was here before mankind it is an independent entity not responsible to anyone, and they are unjudgmental at one with nature. Crystals grow in pegmatites, a space where chemicals help form the minerals that crystals are emanate from. These cavities lie below the earth surface allowing molten rock to form slowly. The molten is known as magma, depending on which chemical it comes into contact with this predicts the size of the stone or crystal.

Period and sapphires are made from iron and magnesium and as we have seen magnesium is also a component of the human cells. Diamonds every girl's best friend come from crystallized forms of pure carbon.

Amethysts are found in cavities of gas bubbles.

Herkimer diamonds are quartz they form in soft mud like rock they focus light and I find them great for cleaning toxins and emotional blockages in those who have become dependent on drugs.

Crystals consist of millions of units of atoms called unit cells these are composed of silicon and oxygen, heat and pressure help to crystallize them making them into different shapes and sizes. Quartz crystals react when pressed or squeezed, they produce a current of electricity similar to the chemical charge of the neurotransmitter in the human body and is one of the main reasons they are successful in the manufacture of television, computers, watches, phones. Perhaps this is one of the reasons that crystals help to balance and harmonise energy in the human body. Whenever the equilibrium of the body is disturbed by the use of ingested chemicals or drugs, crystals are a positive natural way of bringing the body into balance, how easy it is to hold crystal in one's hand and feel the energy return to normal.

These receptive stones can heal the traumatized spirit of the drug user. Like the child who needs a blanket for emotional comfort the methadone taker can hold the crystal which then gives support, this belief alone is a positive affirmation like a payer it grave rates hope in the methadone takers direction, hope generated from the object that instils confidence and a feeling of control. Crystals, do not judge, gives unconditional love, independence, allowing healing on the emotional level.

These transformers of energy are thought to work on the endocrine system where chemicals or hormones are secreted into the blood stream Reiki, Acupuncture, work in the same manner. By surrounding yourself with crystals you allow the imbalance to right itself regenerating the positive energy needed to fight stress and chemical imbalances of daily life. I am always taken aback whenever I see someone on methadone struggle to overcome their dependency on opium.

Something as simple as a crystal can kick start the body and mind into wanting change, by transforming the energy they create balance and balance means contentment and change. I am never surprised to hear how those on large doses of this manufactured opium we call green diesel(methadone) have suddenly come to a decision that they want to detox, following the receiving of a crystal. The awareness of the self has come to the fore and they take control of their lives.

So how are these wonderful rocks formed, our earth is reported to be 4.6 billion years. The Earth's crust is 0.4% of the planet's mass, almost all of this rock is crystalline, and as stated above these are formed of oxygen and silicone. Other elements such as aluminium, iron, calcium, sodium, potassium, and magnesium.

As we see the formation of rocks and crystals are made with the same minerals and chemical components as the human cell.

The earth's crust not only makes mountains but it creates stress fractures in this surface changing and creating many of the earth's minerals by pressure or heat. It is these conditions that allows for the crystallization of minerals. For many thousands of years gems, rocks and stones have left Humans in awe. These are important in our everyday lives because whenever you sit down to watch your colour television it is these crystals that have impurities and emit light that you have to thank for the visions on you TV.

Research by Marcel Vogel a scientist discovered that if he projected his thoughts into a crystal before it became solid the crystal suddenly took the shape of his thought. He maintained that crystals are used in radio stations to communicate; quartz is ground to give the desired frequency.

According to Vogel our thoughts vibrate like a magnetic field oscillation acts like atomic forms of oxygen, nitrogen causing a vibration sensation sending a series of patterns that move outward and around the body. When we think we generate a pattern which in turn oscillates and radiates field that acts on matter. The next time you need to know the time remember your watch is made from quartz crystal ensuring you do not miss your appointment. Crystals are reported to have an electrical current or can change shapes according to light. Crystals can encourages to have positive thoughts, counsellors work in a similar Manner allowing their clients to acknowledge and learn that negative thought patterns are holding them back from achieving their full potential. A growing awareness concerning crystals and healing is on the increase. They have played a major role in history from the pharaohs to the Incans temples. The earth's crusts contain fossilized plants, animals, minerals all compounds and crystal structures, certain tribes used crystals to cure certain illnesses and disease. Emeralds were known to cause diahorea; Rubies were renowned to be a cure for liver problems, while Amethysts were an antidote for snake bites.

Irish kings were inaugurated sitting on a large rock of Granit. Gems were used to decorate the crowns of world kings or queens, the Egyptians carved messages on stones leaving a wealth of history for later scholars to decipher.

Carnelian, Jasper, lapis lazuli was also used to symbolize the sun god. Mountains are seen as sacred and spiritual places. The Cherokee tribe believed that crystals held a powerful healing power and still have crystal skulls, one of those is held in the British museum Cleopatra, used crystals for inner and outer health, crystals are made up of atoms that have bonded together to form patterns, these can grow to large sizes and form from a gas or liquid solution at the correct temperature and pressure, it is important when choosing your crystal to pick the one that you are attracted to as these may be the ones that are in tune with the energy within your body. I have no credible explanation as to how certain crystals seem to work, what I have become aware of in my line of work is that our emotion can have a great effect on our minds just like eating the correct nutritional diet one that is essential for the protein essential fats, vitamins and minerals that enable us to be of sound mind and body. As we have moved into a world of drugs we have lost the wisdom of traditional methods of healing. Our body is built from thousands of different molecules each with vibratory pattern proteins, enzymes all have bio magnetic fields and electrical charged neurotransmitters and receptors inked and interconnected to other parts of the body. Stress causes hormones to be released altering the whole chemical system crystals can maintain a constant electromagnetic at vibration level, if a drummer in a band plays off key, the remaining group shall have to strive to keep the music intact, our body has an electromagnetic field generated by the chemical electrical processes in the body, it is sensitive to the environment, illness can occur when patterns that do not belong to us can disturb our field pattern. Stress is one kind of imbalance that sets of a chain of events disturbing the equilibrium of our body. Continuous stress is like a volcano waiting to explode. Trauma, pollutants, chemicals, can push us into a state of disharmony. Crystals, Reiki, Meditation, visualisation and oils all help to relieve stress thus allowing the energy structure of the body to self- repair. Sleep and dreaming have a similar effect, in order to maintain a body in harmony we must learn ways to eliminate stress whenever it arises. Stress or prolonged stress is rampant in those on methadone; evidence suggests that the methadone individual does best on a program that offers support counselling, respect, independence, education, life skills all associated

Balancing the Chakras

Whenever our body is out of zinc ,or we suffer a dip in energy it is usually felt as coolness, if we are over energized the body has the opposite effect like a pressure cooker we experience an excess of some kind, a feeling of turbulence. We know something is not right but we fail to place our finger on the cause.

Crystal healing picks up on this imbalance and because it does not involve chemicals, or prescribed medication it is harmless to the person receiving it. Crystals work by helping the methadone user's body to function more effectively and natural way. Like Reiki it works on the Etheric body which is where the cells and organs lie. Acupuncture also deals with the meridian system as the Etheric body is interconnected and integrated with the physical.

The emotional body contains all the feelings and emotions, some call this our Aura because it is believed it contains colours of energy that alter and change with our moods. I have seen this with someone on cocaine the aura is clouded in a thick grey colour. All our psychological sensitivities stability lies in the emotional field.

The mental body, these are our thoughts, and cognitive processes. Information processing, perception, all fall under the mental process. Whenever we live surrounded with negative self doubts, lack self-confidence, we can be perceived as suffering from a blockage of energy in this body. Our upbringing as children and belief structure is associated here. The Astral body, this is the forth layer containing our personality, relationships, and our

relationship with humanity.

The next layer is connected to the collective unconscious the sixth level is the universal energy, while the seventh is said to represent the spiritual body.

Crystals that work best on the psychical body are Tourmaline, said to repair bones or muscles it is valuable for Methadone users as most have brittle bones following years of heroin abuse, which has depleted calcium.

As a means of protection I find black Tourmaline of great assistance in grounding, as is black hematite. Pink Tourmaline can produce positive and negative charges at each end it is a great balancer for the Etheric body.

Carnelian I find a motivating stone, it helps disrupt feelings of envy, brings feelings of joy, happiness, stimulates courage, self confidence, ambition, helps methadone users to speak out and assert themselves.

Used above the navel it encourages courage to deal with denial. This stone is also valuable in dealing with infections which many of those on methadone deal with due to hepatitis. I find it wonderful stone for balancing my thyroid which is underactive.

The emotional body like crystals associated with changing mood. Like the weather our mood can be affected by emotions, loss of employment, relationships, family. Smoky, quartz is unemotional helper, it helps calm emotional storms, cleansing, stabilizes, and heals, reduces stress and trauma, all part and parcel of a methadone lifestyle. Stress is a condition of a negative belief about oneself that one is incapable of coping with a given situation. Reality kicks in with this beautiful stone.

Clear quartz helps clear and balance the mind and upper mental processes.

Rose quartz helps with self love and therefore self-confidence.

Turquoise and lapis lazuli settles the mind, strengthen the body as the methadone renews their spiritual awaking. This crystal is a great protective stone, helping to ward off depression that dreaded black negative cloud that sits above the head weighing a ton of bricks...this beautiful stone helps in that it advances the wisdom of those on methadone allowing agreater understanding and clarity of their actions. It returns truth and integrity to its wearer. Malachite is a wonderful green stone, enhancing calmness, patience, inner peace, and teeth .methadone users suffer from calcium deficient's which was mooted upon in the first capture(with a reference to not a molar in their heads.) It is also know to be a treatment for cholera, but I would not encourage that any of these stones be used for internal use.

Fluorite helps develop spiritual awareness, as drugs close down the spirit this stone is wonderful to carry on your person. Purple white and green it symbolizes unconditional love, responsibility, and universal love.

All attributes lacking in today's world.

Unconditional love is always lacking in the lives of drug use.

Amethyst this delightful crystal of purple is a must for the methadone user, not only does it purify, but its powerful healing energy clams emotional violence and anger. As most of the anger is internalised in those who abuse drugs this stone enhances strength. It shall help the sleepless methadone taker to get a proper slumber allowing the regeneration of body and mind, while awaking the spiritually needed to fight drugs.

Aquamarine, shall help smooth, calm, bring tranquillity to the over active mind of the methadone user. It is important in that it dispels negativity, anxiety, all part and parcel of methadone use. By cleansing the glands which are part of the endocrine system it creates balance in the body. Also a protective stone it is useful in helping its wearer to stay off drugs. Colours are important in choosing crystals because different colours are associated with different chakra

Red belongs to the base chakra or energy centres, legs, lips, feet, base or spine are associated with red blood, red is also associated with inflammation pain, swelling, self- confidence, aggression, arrogance, an imbalance of energy at the root chakra can indicate, a lack in, drive, vulnerability, and an inability to set boundaries, red stones are Garnet, Ruby, Jasper, Hematite and Granite.

Creativity is associated with orange most methadone users are creative as most of their art is witness. Orange vibrations help with creativity by removing blockages, energy at the social chakra it is connected to the large intestines and kidneys which are associated with detoxification, by placing amber topaz, orange calcite below the navel it helps release blockages. Methadone is a toxin, orange helps to cleanse the organs of toxins,

Yellow is like serotonin it is a happy colour, by maintaining harmony at the solar plexus the digestive system important in assimilating nutrients from our food intake. A powerful stone and colour for those suffering from coelic disease. Yellow is important for these on methadone as it encourages and strengthens not only the nervous system but helps with clarity around eating habits. Fear is a negative emotion most of those on methadone have in abundance, yellow is lacking in those when fear is present, choices can only surface when fear is revealed, by using or placing yellow stones such as, lemon quartz this can help dispel fear prompting a more positive lifestyle.

Green is the colour of healing it is linked to the heart lungs, arms, hands, growth and change,

Because coming off heroin or methadone entails not only strength but change which is the most important hurdle that methadone users must overcome, it is a day by day struggle to survive, these on methadone have blocked energy due to years of desperation, failed families and relationships, separations, depression, lost opportunities they have guilt around their heart as thick as the walls that protect Fort Knox. Emotionally green stones such as Aventurine, Emerald, and Calcite placed on or near the heart helps to release blocked energy. Green is the colour of Archangel Rachael and personal growth.

Blue is for communication, Turquoise is blue by placing it near the throat it can help with the flow of communication, expression, learning, acceptance, understanding, empathy, communicating is essential for most methadone individuals it helps them to move forward, anger, frustration, self expression are lacking in methadone users. Most have experienced exclusion, from society, may have done a stint in goal emotional detachment is part and parcel of heroin abuse.

Group therapy, Counselling, are enhanced when blue stones like lapis lazuli are placed on a work surface.

Violet is a colour I love because it connects with brain function, especially to the pituitary and pineal glands these two glands lay at the top of the head and between the eyes. The pituitary is the over lord of the endocrine system which indirectly affects the activity of the cell groups in the body. These chemicals are referred to as chemicals. They work by pulling the appropriate hormone molecules from the bloodstream and into the cell. This complex system of chemicals is controlled by the pituitary .Stress (fear, anxiety, pain all contribute to the release of corticotrophin from the hypothalamus setting off a string of action leading to (ACTH) to help us deal with the stressful events. Placing a violet crystal between the eyes has the added benefit of relaxing you bringing down stress levels.

Pink: found at the heart, it is known also to help in releasing stress, improve with self image, tolerance, trauma, burning pink candles or placing pink stones in a room of methadone users can help to calm the anxiety, depression, stress the symptoms that cling to the methadone user. And which is tied to the overall issues of emotional issues, death, loss of employment, divorce, economical difficulties illness extended family emotional healing can be helped by a number of ways.

Doctors issue prescriptions for depression, give diazepam for anxiety, these wonderful healers deal in drugs, holistic methods include Relaxation, Reiki, Meditation, Yoga are now getting a better rating from those that deal in science only, theory is a great tool but only until another bright spark disproves or proves the previous theory, emotional imbalance can only be seen to be healed by the giving of medication, manmade drugs that reap massive profits for the chosen few. The power of Crystals like natural grasses, plants, trees ,flowers have flown to the four winds of history as scientific theory has taken centre stage in the healing of the human race.

Chakras are located along the nerves and lymphatic tissues and endocrine glands; a chakra is the location where a multitude of Different influences interact with the human being. Chakras transmit life energy into the body which is distributed into the remained of the physical body from each chakra point through a number of nerves known as meridians. If stress accumulates in certain chakra's energy builds up disturbing other chakras this contributes to illness.

Pink or Green is the colours of the heart which rules emotion by placing rose quartz at the centre of the chest as the heart rules All balance and equilibrium by pumping blood around the body so it is important that the heart charka is balanced. We know when this misbalanced as we are assertive, can cope, stay calm and don't become aggressive. The opposite occurs when the heart Chakra is out of balance we doubt our own self- worth, need reassurance, and become intolerant we also suffers from guilt. Methadone takers Suffer with many of these symptoms especially hopelessness, low self esteem and heaps of stress. I find in my reiki sessions that by placing a rose quartz at the heart centre not only does the client breath more easier but can suddenly open up and want to discuss some past trauma one that is contributing to blocked energy, the natural flow of energy into the Environment helps the methadone individual to let go and move forward by transmitting their ideas, thoughts and fears, they feel relieved. Methadone use occurs in most underprivileged communities. Communities that live in close proximity to family members extended cousins, aunts, uncles, sisters, brothers, mothers and fathers, when illness occurs it is played out like a Greek drama. Everyone is pulled into the act, gossip is ripe, when a death occurs but gossip is negative where as doing is positive. Negative feedback is quite destructive, it is energy less, has nothing to contribute, it is stuck or stagnated like a vase flowers that set in the same water for two weeks, and they wilt and die. Methadone use is stagnation; it is like being stuck in mud, a whirlpool always trying to keep their heads from sinking below. The drama of living and coping is great. Most Remain in the communities they were born into surrounded by drama and illness that is curable by drugs, by looking outside them for the cure they give away personal power that comes from within. Crystals contribute to rebalancing the electromagnetic energy field that embodies all life on the planet even the human aura.

What's that smell?

This question pops up every time I do group therapy, counselling or teach. The fragrances wafting below the ceiling clinging to the sense receptors in the nose. Essential oils come from plants, flowers, herbs. The crease on the foreheads of the clients which resembles corrugated tin assures me that I am seen as a little bit mad. We are unaware of the medicines made by our ancestors our perception is that drugs are made and sold in the chemists shop. We only have to examine old text books to learn how our ancestors used certain plants, flowers or herbs to cure illness and while some plants are still used in certain medications most have been lost to us Herbs were either used to kill germs or were infused and used as concoctions' for certain illnesses. We know this from history when we read how Red Hugh O'Donnell and Hugh O Neill Irelands Kings kept herbalists in their service. These men of learning would travel the country-side picking and making the medicines of the day that cured anything from poisoning to a bunion. This was demonstrated daily as each king of the region employed doctors to administer their secret herbs to attend to the wounds of returning armies... Pine cones were burnt to help clean a room of infection as was the lavender bush, because it had healing properties. Willow was given to help digestive problems and is today the main ingredients in aspirin. These changes came about because natural resources are difficult to control due to all kinds of weather conditions and population growth and science; we have resorted to and become dependent on chemical cocktails that don't appear to include the many compondants found in the natural environment. The thousands of years it took our ancestors to try and test the materials used to treat infection, cuts, illness have all disappeared leaving artificial chemical molecules to replace them.

Essential oils and humans have a similar make up, we are chemical oils are made from plants, we need plants to breath, cells from plants have DNA humans have individual DNA structures, we both depend on natural chemicals to function Trees can produce chemicals known as tannins which are known to kill anything that attacks It.

Perhaps Prince Charles wasn't as daft as some thought when he said we should hug trees. Dr. David Rhodes from Washington University reported that some trees such as the willow and alder can send chemical messages or hormones like humans into the atmosphere; it appears those trees have a life of their own. Our ancestors would have known every plant, tree, flower bank needed to restore health in a time of great warfare. By picking a flower early in the morning or at a certain noon time, they 101could avail of all the chemical goodness needed for their work.

The word chemistry means plant juice these can be extracted and made into essential oils through the process of distilling, the flowers, grasses, roots, and leaves are all gathered dried and made into wonderful fragrance. Essential oils are taken into the body by absorption via the skin, or by the nose so they can activate the receptor cells starting a chain of events in the brain our nose detects smell by means of the olfactory nerve endings which transmit this information to the olfactory bulb in the brain which conveys sensation of smell, as nerve impulses to the brain the receptors in the membrane detect smells ending Signals along the nerve fibres. The aroma from essential oils reaches the brain. Those on heroin or methadone or cocaine shall inform you that the smell of anything associated with their drug abuse is enough to send them hankering after a past drug lifestyle. . Our bodies are made from amino acids from the protein we consume manufactured into these amino acids; the series of chemicals needed to change the neurotransmitters receptors is staggering. The brain is a powerhouse of complexity. Many drugs enter the brain immediately passing the blood brain barrier, essential oils are reported to work in a similar manner we smell, they absorb them through the skin in aromatherapy, but to date no individual has explained how or why these wonderful aromas work only that they do. Perhaps they affect the enzymes which are proteins that regulate the chemical reaction in the body. We have thousands of enzymes each with its own chemical structure. Enzyme activity while influenced by many factors can be increased or inhibited by certain drugs. It is believed that essential oils can cause a change in the calcium ion which carries an electrical change.

However, these oils work to enhance mood or behaviour, as I am not a scientist I cannot answer that question, like crystals which can help heal certain conditions especially emotional ones, oils appear to work in addiction. Drug addiction if it be heroin, methadone, cocaine, hash or the vast range of prescribed drugs for depression, anxiety stress all connected to emotional issues. The methadone user has replaced one opium for another addiction. Withdrawals are similar individuals cannot come off by themselves they must be under a doctor's supervision. Oils that can help with withdrawal symptoms and should be used in a safe environment are a mixture of basil bergamot, clearly Sage, Vetiver. I find this a great helper by spraying it into the room before group therapy.

Valerie Ann wormwood in her book the fragment mind gives essential information regarding the history and use of these Wonderful aromas. Emotional shock can be treated with Rose Otto Neroli Mandarin. Memory loss is helped with Sandalwood, Camomile, Cypress, Lemon, Orange, and Bergamot.

Methadone individuals as stated many times have difficulty dealing with the gigantic stressors they encounter in their everyday life. This can manifest itself in a number of ways, anger, aggression, fear, sleeplessness, Restlessness. Essential oils like lavender, chamomile, and celery sage are useful in dealing with stressful situations.

Loss of a loved one, separation is also felt as a loss and as many fathers are separated from family members or children. They have the added guilt to add to the mix. Mixing Lavender, Cypress benzioin is a good starter for those who are grieving especially due to suicide. Putting a few drops of Rose Otto, Neroli Benzioin, Vetiver onto a room burner works wonders for drugs users especially as they struggle to leave a drug lifestyle behind. The person coming off opium not only needs to change a lifestyle, but they go through a grieving process. Some drug abusers have indulged themselves in a cloak of denial from a tender age; some may have started using as young as fifteen years old. Their emotional growth is stunted, they are losing a friend, someone who has102 gotten them through trauma, that was always there, a crutch. All reality could be wiped out, the heroin didn't intrude into their lives, it didn't judge, they were in control. No one had informed them that they could solve many stressful situations by simple solutions and relaxing techniques that have been around since time began.

By simply placing some oils in a room they could ensure a helpful assistance in overcoming their problem.

The timid orange or yellow Marigold sunbathing on the patio could help heal wounds, stimulate circulation, athlete's foot, cleanse boils, and help constipation a common complaint with those on methadone.

1. Horse chestnut was carried in past times and seen as protecting its carrier. Spanish farmers are reported to feed it to cattle as a means of increasing milk production. Herbs took centre stage in the reign of Queen Elizabeth and her Father Henry the Eight, Elizabeth had honey suckle sprinkled on the stone slabs that covered the palace floor ,so as to perfume the room ,this clever tactic ensured that the stale smells did not penetrate into her bedroom keeping her awake or causing infection Garlic: eaten by the international community has a lasting effect on cholesterol by lowering it, this stringent bulb is also a great healer of the dreaded athletes foot by rubbing it on the affected area it kills the fungi These also protect strawberries, beetroot, and other vegetables from certain pests. A wonderful way to stop the need for pesticides fungicides and other chemical spaying. Individuals on methadone tend to have a lot of anger. Essential oils that can help disperse this negative frustration is a combination of Chamomile, Rose Moroc, Black pepper; I mix these in a little water and place in a burner. Anxiety: another negative emotion can be helped by mixing some Bergamot, Lavender, Patchouli oil, make in a similar way with water, or spray about the room, or on the clothing of the sufferer and watch as anxiety evaporates.

Depression: can be helped by oils such as Black pepper, Basil, Bergamot. Spray in every room and wait to see if the symptoms associated with depression evaporate, these are feeling joyless, sad, worthlessness, guilt. If not then seek a doctor's advice if depression lasts for long periods the sufferer may need medication to get them over the problem.

It is my belief that mild depression which is usually brought about by emotional problems is best treated by going to a counsellor, or a good friend who shall listen. Grief: losing a loved one is a daunting task that is not easily overcome. Death is an individual experience and no too losses are the same. As humans we deal with pain in our own way, and working through pain is not easy. But we can use Essential oils to help. Oils comfort us, because they are inhaled and have a beautiful aroma and they also work on the neurotransmitters.

Use uplifting oils such as Neroli, Patchouli, a delightful smell, Melissa. You can do this in a number of ways, either burn a candle placing a few drops of oil unto the melted wax, or perform the above method of mixing the oils in water and spraying, or drop three or four drops of each oil unto a tissue and carry in a pocket of handbag.

Drugs: Is the new curse in society, they are causing untold mental problems. Mental illness like psychosis, manic depression, depression can be attributed to the increase in drug use. Extreme mood swings are a growing concern for families who have been torn apart by the drug culture. Manic depression and drug induced psychosis is on the increase as communities struggle to deal with the behaviour associated with these conditions. While these serious conditions can and should be treated by a doctor there is a lot that the sufferer can do.

We must first recognize that the condition can be helped by nutrition, essential fatty acids vitamins (B3) which was discussed in earlier captures.

It is now recognized that certain neurotransmitters are responsible for the imbalance in the body. Oils that do seem to help are Chamomile Roman, Frankincense, lavender, Sandalwood, Patchouli,

When someone is suffering from this condition they can use different oils for the different stages.

The manic stage the user should only use one oil on its own.

This can be

Lavender

Neroli

Chamomile

The depressive stage should indulge the beautiful smelling Rose, place a few drops in a warm bath, or on the sleeves of a Jumper, or on a burner with water that you use on a regular basis.

You can also dilute 30 ml of almond oil as a base to three of four drops of the above oil and Massage into your body following a bath.

To dispel self loathing mix base oil with rose Otto or geranium.

Guilt: follows the methadone user like a pair of unfitting gloves, I find that whenever I need to expel feelings of Guilt from the room that a combination of nutmeg, vetiver, Jasmine does the trick. You can follow the same procedure as before, either by spraying in the atmosphere or burning in a burner, always ensure that you extinguish all live flames.

Schizophrenia: I work with a number of people who suffer with this disorder and are struck by the strength and courage needed to survive. Seen as dangerous or mad the sufferer must endure a barrage of medication as a means of leading a normal existence. Symptoms include confused thinking processes, hearing voices, neglect of personal hygiene, and exclusion from reality. As I use essential oils in my everyday work with those suffering from Schizophrenia I find that the oils best suited are Lavender, Rose Otto, Lemon, and Geranium Spray in the air or on the seats that the sufferer is sitting on, As the Schizophrenia I deal with are recovering heroin abusers and are on methadone I also find that the oils used for drug withdrawal work in a positive manner especially when mixed with Rose Otto. Like crystals some essential oils ground and counteract negative emotions such as depression, Anxiety, mood swings, stress, egotistical.

Patchouli not only grounds it also helps lift spirit, it allows freedom from restrictions and as we all know methadone dulls the complete personality.

Essential oils free the addictive personality from a habit of viewing drugs as a means to an end. Heroin and methadone are not one and the same but never the less they are both opiates, both hold the mind, body and spirit hostage to a negative lifestyle. They rob the individual of independence and freedom, they create dependency, block reality, destroy families, separate loved ones and cause much suffering and emotional pain for the user.

As stated earlier in this book the only difference being that heroin is illegal and lasts from three to four hours before the next fix is needed, while methadone also comes from morphine is legal, lasts twenty four hours and the user doesn't have to knock your granny over the head to rob her handbag to feed his or her habit. It is society's way of staying positive and safe in the knowledge that they can sleep in their beds.

Natural Companions

Herbs are not new to Europe and findings suggest that seeds from certain herbs were found in Stone Age settlements. As someone who has had a heighten interest in herbal medicine possibly due to a link to ancestors who had a knowledge in this skilled craft. Intrigued by the wild plants and flowers that adorn our country -side and a love of nature I sat about researching this fascinating subject that is all but lost in today's world.

Cultivating herbs is a wonderful past time, and it is an interesting past time, one that can absorb your attention for hours on end.

Herbs have a long history most of which was recorded in parchments by scribes who usually were monks, especially trained in monasteries.

Some of these works were the foundation of modern medicine and some plants or trees are combined to make some of the tables in the shelves of supermarkets.

Herbalists had the knowledge about which plant, flower or shrub could heal infections, disease, and other less known illness that afflicts us today.

The Greek scientists Hippocrates and Galen well know herbalists, who left writings that advanced medicine as we know it today.

Their works were developed and enriched by Arab scientists.

It wasn't until the 16 century that Physical directory written by Nicholas Culpeper's informative words detailing the important effects that plants and scrubs were in the fight against

disease that herbalists and their significance became renowned.

By the eighteenth century science was on the march and holistic knowledge had to take a back seat as a German apothecary began to experiment making the fascinating discovery that the sap from the humble poppy be manufactured into morphine, and the rest is history.

The active agent of certain plants and herbs became the end product.

Reduced to chemical form downgraded as the wholeness and importance of the plant was lost in the stampede of science.

Plants have a cell structure, they need sun, water, and light to survive like humans some will only thrive in certain soils while others are hardy and survive in shady places.

Like humans plants grow when they receive attention, love, respect, and like humans we all share the same planet.

Herbs are a wonderful source of nutrition a natural companion for any meal. Easy to grow and maintain they produce as little problem as an indoor plant.

It is important to learn which herbs are beneficial and which ones we should avoid, but a growing interest in herb growing has sparked a more intellectual approach to knowing which herbs we can use and those we need to avoid.

As this book centres on a new approach to methadone and incorporates nutrition I have concentrated on vegetables, which anyone can grow in pots or window boxes.

As Hippocrates remarked "let your food be medicine and your medicine be food".

When I mention vegetables whose health depends on the soil they grow in, in the 15 th century in Ireland the land was cultivated with sand and seaweed, no pesticides or fungicides for our ancestors it was all organic compost.

These wise men recognised that vegetables grown under such conditions provided the greater amount of vitamins and minerals and trace elements such as zinc that is missing in the 20 century diet due to depleted soil.

As a child I would be sent to pick the fresh onions, lettuce, tomatoes and potatoes all slumbering next to the blackberry, raspberry, gooseberry bushes in the back garden.

That special taste is not evident in super market food as it must undergo the process of chemical dunking to ensure it had a shelf life.

Those on methadone are a walking chemical time bomb as they pump opium, chemical laden processed food, vegetables that have their heads douched in chemicals, deep-fried food, the list is endless.

The need for information on what we are pumping into the methadone body in the name of advancement needs a closer examination.

As methadone takers are prone to have weakened immune systems it is imperative to educate them on organic foods that shall enhance their overall health.

For a healthy immune system the body must receive a daily amount of vitamins, minerals, and trace elements which should but is not available in the processed food provided on the supermarket shelf it is and can be supplies in foods grown and cultivate in organic soil.

For someone on methadone to eat a diet high in food that has undergone the rigors of constant pesticides and insecticides which does not take rocket science to realise is a health hazard and can only add to a liver over laden with chemicals is like flying a plane without an engine.

Could it be that those who fill our shops with chemically produced foods

Have little fore-sight as to the danger of destroying our immune systems, or perhaps they need to read Marcel Vogel on how man and plants are living objects, who can pick up on the sensitive energy fields around them, by feeding their own force field they feed energy back to earth.

Can you imagine if Vogel is correct in his assumption how it must feel to have tons of chemicals poured over your person a number of times a year.

Chemicals cling to the leaves and stalks of vegetables it would take a lot of washing to dispel all residue, but the story does not end there the battered plant must endure a barrage of dipping into another chemical to dress it for the shelf so some nice house wife shall find it attractive and healthy looking enough so as to feed her children.

When the teacher suspects that her child could be suffering from ADHD the mother almost loses her reason running around like a headless chicken full of guilt and loss as to how she has a child with an affliction. The demented woman is unaware that her Childs cognitive system and neurotransmitters could be sensitive to the many chemicals roaming our supermarkets in the name of profit.

The good old wild leek is beyond recognition as it under- went a makeover With advanced husbandry, leeks were renowned for their medicinal influence for someone who was a diabetic Leek extract is a wonderful smoother for someone who is unfortunate to come in contact with a grandchild who has chicken pots ending up with painful shingles. Medicine for this condition costs as much as 100 Euros where-as. a wild leek dabbed on the affected area can relieve the pain, but I must add never undertake to treat yourself before first consulting your doctor .Carrots are not only an antioxidant but they are brilliant to eat if you have anything wrong with your liver or gallbladder. Containing vitamin A they are a must in every dinner menu. Matched with leeks and onions they are said to expel worms especially thread worms a common occurrence in some children fed a diet of sweets and a sign that the immune system needs strengthening. These hardy orange vegetables can be grown without much assistance; I grow mine in an old wash basin at the side of the house. Any old container will do the trick. Now we cannot leave out the cabbage, the dreaded cabbage I revered to it as a child, I would turn up my nose as my mother drank the smelly water left over from boiling, the liquid that had escaped the kitchen sink.

A rick source of calcium the cabbage is a must for many methadone users, years of heroin abuse has depleted their calcium so what better way to restore this much needed mineral but to eat

Cabbage.

My mother had the correct idea as she never suffered from brittle bones even though it was in the family.

Cabbage is invaluable for placing on a festered cut as it draws out the infection leaving it clean, by placing a cabbage leaf on a headache it shall relieve the pain. Horses that suffer from hoof rot can be treated with a heated cabbage leaf wrapped around the swollen area.

For those on methadone many suffer from an over worked liver and this causes headaches, by heating a few cabbage leaves and placing them on the area they should get some natural relieve

And healing as cabbage can pull harmful substances such as toxins from tissues.

When we examine the documents of the seventeenth century we can see how important the humble cabbage was, it worked by drawing out the poison from the affected area.

When we tell our children to eat their greens we are usually passing on the information we received from our own parents without having full knowledge why. Spinach was something Popeye ate to impress his girlfriend Olive, every tin he backed down his neck his muscles burst through his shirt.

But spinach is rich in all the vitamins and minerals that make up the human calls, calcium, potassium, magnesium, iron, vitamins A, B, C, in this one vegetable we are ensuring that the essential foods are feeding our neurotransmitters and cells. A salad made with baby spinach Leaves, diced carrots and fresh basil and parsley are a tonic for the methadone user.

One important role of spinach in the diet of those on green diesel is its function in helping to cleanse the bowel, most methadone takers suffer from constipation, by including some leaves in their diet they not only eliminate the problem but ensure that they help their liver and dispel kidney stones.

This natural companion leaves no residue or side effects as does medication. Lettuce sits proudly on every table once summer peeps its head through over cast sky; its beautiful light green compliments the rosy tomato and darker spring onions at every barque in the world. This delicious healthy vegetable if grown organically will provide you with vitamins A. B. and C more importantly you get the benefit t of sodium, magnesium, and Iron.

Insomnia is a problem for those on methadone; some suffer so bad that sleeping pills are the only answer as sleep deprivation can be dangerous. Lettuce is known to induce sleep. Having planted my vegetables I am delighted to say that the blood red beetroot took centre stage in my list of do's mostly because I love its crunchy taste but mostly because off its properties.

It is invaluable to the digestive system especially constipation and the dreaded haemorrhoids. Recent studies suggest that this hard round vegetable is high on the list of anti- cancer properties. The best way to gain the best from this plant is not to eat it from a jar full of vinegar but to boil it fresh.

Like any vegetable if it is over cooked the precious vitamins and minerals are lost, Its Therapeutic qualities are enormous and beneficial and giving optimum health While most people hate peeling them the simple onion is a humble vegetable My earliest recollections of the healing properties of onions was my mother mixing a sliced onion in warm water and giving some to my sister who continually screamed while pulling her knees up to her chest within one hour she had receive great relieve.

Milk thistle is nothing more than the extract of artichokes an almost neglected vegetable its ability to help protect the liver from excess alcohol .It works by activating the juices and bile that is central to liver function.

Many of those taking daily doses of methadone from 80ml to 120 ml and who suffer from hepatitis which is inflammation of the liver, a sluggish liver can interfere with the brain as the liver is the clearing house of toxins in the body.

Anything that contributes to alleviating elevated toxic levels in methadone takers needs to be taken seriously. As most also consume alcohol eating artichokes or drinking their extraction should be a consideration.

We in Ireland have a love affair with the potato as it was our staple diets for hundreds of years, its failure in 1845caused the worse famine in history wiping out over a million people. There are over 1,600 varieties of the good old spud,

As children we believed that we could get rid of warts if we cut a spud in half, rubbed it on the wart, buried the spud, then wait for a week and the wart would drop off.

Potatoes while providing a source of protein they are mostly a carbohydrate, potato juice is beneficial in the treatment of eczema a skin disorder associated with an allergy. Potatoes are starch therefore is excellent in the treatment of infected cuts, swellings, diabetes. The best part of the spud is just beneath the skin; it is there that most of the goodness lies.

1. Herbs can be used in healing unlike conventional medicine they are natural, receive the sun's rays, and has had a valued place in our past history. Medicine today has become the mother of all treatment. From a head cold to a fart we are prescribes synthetic drugs. This is due partly to how the medical profession is trained and partly to the big bucks made by the pharmaceutical companies. Not to mention the number of clients attending the doctor with trivial complaints. Herbal medicine does not warrant the same money as conventional drugs, they cannot be patterned, whereas drugs can and are produced synthetically from certain herbs and were all conventional medicine arrived from are fetching fast amounts of dollars and Euros for scientific research. The profit it's amassed in the name of medical advancement is staging.

The medical profession does not embrace natural herbs nor does it deal in nutrition except for a few visionaries ahead of their time. Ironically when a patient presents with an emotional problem such as depression due to lack of money and an inability to feed their children they are given a prescription for benso. Nutrition is not a factor nor is the sunken face that lacks the protein needed to make the amino acids to enhance healthy neurotransmitters. The patient is fed a diet of chemicals when a thick chunk of steak or chicken would produce the natural chemicals needed, to fuel the much need good health food without side effects.

All life forms need sun, we cannot survive without it, and plants also have a life form they use light to make energy which conveys energy into matter. Albert Einstein informed us of this when we said, "energy and matter are one and the same, and "one can be converted into the other. A theory long forgotten by some in the medical profession. Perhaps that is why some have great difficulty in understanding homeopathy, acupuncture, Reiki all energy-based holistic medicine.

Conventional drugs are based on isolated chemicals, and are made synthetically while herbal medicines are based on the whole plant and are natural all are energy rich because they are affected by the sun, are slower to work in the body, and have the desired vitamins and minerals missing from synthetic drugs.

Our ancestors would have an olham (doctor) who was versed in the knowledge of every herb, plant and tree that could heal everything from infection, to disease. Herbs could strengthen the immune system, stop infection,

Most grew in the wild like comfrey, this is a great food for insects growing to a height of 5 feet, the young leaves when harvested have valuable proteins, vitamins, tannins, and alkaloids, the leaves can be fried like spinach or used in mulching, animal feed, and fertilizer. Medically they can be used in compresses, sprains, rheumatism. By mixing the roots in brandy you can make a tincture and apply to a sprain or strained muscle.

Coltsfoot this native perennial is best suited to soil with lime and the sun, by picking the flowers in February or March you can dry them.

The young leaves are delicious cooked but like any herb you should not take excessive amounts.

Chives are from the family of onions and garlic, the lilac flowers reach a height of 12 ins and this grass like plant, chives are a treat in a summer salad, the flowers can be used in a bowl of water as a flower arrangement with candles.

Chives have active agents the oils from chives are a great high blood reducer, they contain vitamin C when taken in a sandwich they make a refreshing and healthy snack.

Garlic said to enhance longlivity and planted underneath trees it helps to keep pests of strawberries, and beetroot. Garlic is also good for keeping cholesterol levels down as someone who suffered with high from a level of 7.6 my cholesterol fell to a staging 3.4 naturally after implementing a garlic tablet and one omega 3 in my daily diet. Since that discovery my son has also brought down his cholesterol and has now off his statins, this cholesterol helper can cause liver damage as any GP or instructions on the package shall inform you.

Not only has garlic antibiotic properties which I use to its full advantage by crushing garlic and rubbing if over my work surface to kill germs, but I have cut my cleaning bills by half. Garlic has other uses because it can treat worm infestation; the Greeks are reported to treat tumours with garlic, as did the Romans. This round white pungent bulb, did not receive any medals for the lives it saved during the wars, its ability to stop infections in the badly wounded went unrecorded by the medical profession perhaps the reason being the humble garlic bulb does not have an inflated ego. The crushed bulb was smeared around the wound hence keeping the infection at bay.

The medical profession are now standing up and acknowledging the importance of this wonderful natural healer as its intricate complex structure is playing a part in keeping cancer at arm's length.

Garlic oil contains Allicin that destroys bacteria like lavender and eucalyptus oil they can help fight the MRSA which has hit our hospital wards invading open wounds and is now know to be responsible for certain deaths.. By mixing these three oils together we as a society can play our part in the protection of our own health.

By planting some garlic in tubs on the patio we can not only cut out the middle man but grow pure garlic that had not had its head drowned in chemicals.

The hepatitis and HIV methadone sufferer can have chemical free antibiotics at hand.

Garlic also kills of athlete's foot; it stops the itching faster than any cream on the market. By rubbing the crushed garlic over the infected area while it is a little uncomfortable it is worth the effort.

1f you are worried about the odour garlic leaves on the breath you can chew some fresh parsley .this removes the smell and is a bonus.

Echinacea those who have abused heroin and are now on methadone suffer from a low immune systems

Echinacea is a wonderful immune enhancer as it helps fight infection, whenever our body believes itself to be under attack it sends white blood cells called macrophages which when activated cells to attack the infection before it reaches other cells. Because it helps the immune system to defeat viral infections it is a must for those on methadone of course I also advocate that the patients consults their doctor first.

Eczema also afflicts many methadone users Echinacea is a useful tool in the containment of this condition, it is also recommended that it is the sign of an allergen which appears to more prevalent in those taking methadone a fact that may explain away why allergies may play a role in addiction

Honey. The healing properties of honey are now well founded, perhaps due to its anti microbial compounds, trace elements, vitamins C and a and the wonder family of B vitamins that is essential for good mental health and according to new research is lacking in those suffering with depression.

Honey also plays a role in healing those ugly ulcers that afflict the elderly. Bedsores obtained by lying in the one position for long periods can benefit t from the use of honey, its ability to keep

The wound from infection occurs due to the drying effects of the honey.

Flu symptoms can by eliminated by adding a few spoonfuls of honey to water used to boil oranges and lemons.

This excellent tonic will have the flu bug on the hop in pronto time, without the chemicals. Honey is also high in the antibacterial hydrogen peroxide and formic acid. Over all honey is invaluable for infections. Bedsores, colds, flu, burns, and a helping of vitamins, it is also safe provided you are not allergic to stings. Bee hives are usually sat near trees while the beautiful intelligent creatures fly long distant to gather the neuter for the queen bee. In recent years a strain of bees from Africa have managed to reach the shores of America these are more aggressive than

European bees honey is a great healer for burns and ulcers .Its important healing properties are under the scientific microscope as more research is carried out on this wonderful herb.

Tea tree oil is a great flee and head lice fighter, by mixing it in dog shampoo it helps protect my dogs from flees. Oil is extracted from the leaves and branches of the tree, found in Australia it were introduced by the army to help fight infection. While its smell has a distinctive strong odder it is revered for its antiseptic properties. It had active chemicals and while not as complex as garlic oil it works on the same premise.

This wonderful anti -microbial is in a league of its own for the natural benefits are a plus for killing those nasty fungi athletes foot, by dabbing a few drops of oil mixed with water on the effect area the tee tree kills the fungi. Dry scalp is a precursor for dandruff by rinsing you hair in warm water with 2 drops of oil you can have shinny hair minus the white spots.

Ringworm is almost extinct, yet when I got my cat from a cat's home it had ring worm this contagious disease has to be treated by washing the cat in tee tree oil for two weeks.

The dreaded lip sore know as herpes can benefit t from a lip balm made with the oil or dab a few drops in a tissue and place it on the area .it shall stop it in its tracks.

The uses for this oil are great, it can be used for chicken pox, and shingles, and it is oil that is used externally only as it is toxic.

I like to burn it in my clinic as a precursor in stopping the spread of colds and infection, like garlic it is a great antiseptic for work tops, be careful if applying it to wooden worktops.

Marigolds

As a maker of organic creams and ointments one of my great delights is the growing and intergrading the beautiful orange or yellow marigolds in creams to counteract skin problems especially eczema. This nasty condition is on the increase especially among children. By mixing bees wax with certain oils and the strained Water from the marigold I get a creamy substance that helps eliminate the terrible itch associated with this condition.

Most doctors prescribe a cream that contains cortisone that thins the skin when used for long periods of time. As I consider this condition to be a result of poor diet and lack of vitamins or minerals, 1 encounter this in my work with those on methadone. The red patches that loiter on elbows, wrists, behind ears is embarrassing for the suffer, cortisone like all chemicals are ingested, absorbed, or sniffed. Eczema returns as soon as the cream is stopped which indicates we need to search for the underlying cause, hot the effect which we get with the cream application. Skin ulcers, wounds, and burns all benefit t gratefully from marigolds.

Infections are a common complaint in those on methadone partly due to a weakened immune system. The cultivation of crops, vegetables, fruits, is a growing concern as the demand to feed growing populous increases. The dangers of pesticides, fungicides, have now come full circle as we become aware of the problems of a lack of trace minerals in the depleted and chemical saturated soil. This is also applicable to prescribed medication and illegal drugs.

Zinc

Zinc is one trace mineral that has almost disappeared from our radar, its deficiency in children and those who have abuse heroin for many years is frightening, methadone as we mentioned in previous chapters plays havoc with the natural bowel movements. Absorption is present whenever loose stools are evident, zinc is important in immunity, our bodies' have enzymes-as

I mentioned in a previous capture it is these enzymes that determined if a neurotransmitter is broken down, or reactivated, whenever a zinc deficiency exits the result is a lack of responses do not function properly, causing retardation, lack of appetite, depression, anxiety, and weakened immune system.

Zinc is an important trace element in methadone takers if they are to fight inflammation of the liver. Hepatitis is a serious condition as the liver is underperforming in some methadone takers. Its protective properties help the methadone taker immune system to fight infection and disease; it contributes to cell building as does the vitamins and minerals we get from food. Research shows that those with HIV/AIDS have lower levels of zinc and it is imperative if they are to fight infection a daily intake of zinc can be of assistance. We get out source of zinc from food especially cereal, meats, whole grain foods and bread, oysters, as the latter is out of the daily budget of the methadone user; a daily intake of zinc is advisable.

Colour me positive

Colour plays a large role in our lives. Its origins are traceable back to the Arabs who had their stalls laid out with multicoloured spices, herbs and fruit. Travel to India ,South America and you shall be fascinated by the bright reds, yellows, pinks, blues, and purples, that jump out at you lifting your mood, giving you that powerful feel good factor Working on a methadone program can at the very least be taxing as negatively lurks in every facet of the user. The dull lifeless eyes, thread worn faces showing years of neglect stare out of sunken socks in their attempt at coping with hopelessness and change. It is only when you get to know each individual that the strength and courage laying beneath those expressionless glances that one can see pride surface giving an insight into the real person. Warm passionate, loving, strong, and intelligent.

As a means of staying positive I choose carefully my colour of clothing to help me to deal with the work that I love. The joy and respect given by those on methadone put others to shame who refuse to look at the person but focus only on the negativity associated with methadone taking.

As mentioned this negativity extends to family members and the community as a whole.

Like lepers in the film Ben Hur they must scurry away from their neighbourhood to attend for their green diesel at a clinic that would not be out of place in the west bank, hopelessness stalks their thin shoulders until they learn that the ignorance shown to their plight is not off their making but in those that refuse to open their eyes to reflect on their own shortcomings..As I keep a watchful eye on the progress of the clients I work with I am struck by their generosity to their fellow humans, their nonjudgmental attitude care and consideration for others they have endured a barrage of insults from others who speak with spiked tongues. Insults also appear in the form of complaints by humans that have not taken the time to listen, who are caught up in the game of blind man's bluff, as their blinkers are firmly glued to their small brains.

As a means of dealing with every day stress and negativity it is vital that those taking methadone

To allow this negativity to bounce of them ,the way to stay positive is an enriched attitude helped by colour, herbs proper nutrition, reiki, acupuncture, meditation, and saying a few healing mantras as we walk through the day. Not only is this confidence building but it helps to deflect the negativity of their dependence on a drug approved by society. What better way to take control of your life than, to know you are making the decisions about how you manage your life and not the substances or prescribed medication that is handed out in the name of detox.

Below I have compiled a list of colours that can be used to build confidence making you feel better about yourself. Colour can also be applied to food, to enhance a healthy eating regime making sure that the methadone taker is taking into their body the correct food needed to fuel both neurotransmitters ,the nervous system, endocrine system all the inter-connecting organs, hormones, cells, immune system vital components of the body

And the vitamins and-minerals needed white preparing them to eliminate toxins leaving a

Liver to work normally ensuring better mental health and a brighter future.

Colours are therapeutic, we all have a colour we like better that others, different colours can energise us, dispel stress, heal or beat depression.

A connection between energy and colour dates back to the ancient civilisation.

Colour healing was introduced by physicians and astrologers as early as the fifteenth century, using crystals and minerals. The e American journal of advanced science maintains that colour can be used to overcome disorders such as addiction, anorexia, depression, anxiety. This breakthrough shows how far we have moved away from natural harmony by seeking out drugs as a means of healing disturbed energy flow.

Pink is a wonderful healing colour due to its association with love, In order to heal we first must let go of the distrust and hurt that binds us to the past.

This magnetic colour can release you from negativity concerning yourself, enhance confidence and build bridges to those that have disowned us due to drugging. It can have a calming effect in times of great stress dispelling hostility, and anxiety. Help bonding with children, acquire affection and love. It is a clam cool colour, can indicate you are strong, independent, creative, steadfast trustworthy, good at handling finances and fair.

Pink will allow you to nurture and believe that your goats are attainable not to berate yourself if you fall back; it lets the methadone user to be gentle allowing the self made stone wall to be removes slowly so that they come off in their own time.

Methadone users should burn some rose oil before going to sleep making sure to put out all naked flames. By placing a few drops in some water and sprinkling it about the sitting room it helps dispel any arguments and stress for the occupants. Be careful as love will be in the air so take percussions if you don't want a pregnancy as pink is the colour of fertility. Fruit associated with pink are raspberries, these contain vitamin c and for methadone takers they are a natural immune booster, cleaning the toxins from the liver thus allowing for better cognition function.

Raspberries mixed with cranberry juice makes delicious smoothies.

This early morning energizing drink contributes to a healthy start for the methadone user. Pink grapefruit juice can be squeezed and drank, it is rich in vitamin C and potassium can be beneficial for diabetes, sore throats and contains anti-oxidising, as most methadone users smoke pink grapefruit is a must.

Like the ordinary grapefruit it is delicious heated under the grill for a light snack with a little honey.

Rhubarb once grew in the wild, this hardy plant needs little attention as it grows in thick clumps. Its stalks are a pink- red this wonderful cheap plant contains oxalic acid, like beetroot, spinach it eliminates toxins from the cells allowing the methadone user to cut down on a build-up of dangerous levels in the body.

It contains most of the minerals needed for cell structure ,vitamin A, C,Potassium, manganese, calcium which is a rich source of getting calcium into the body to replenish calcium loss without the need for medicine.

Orange is the colour associated with the chakra below the navel, by wearing this colour the individual on methadone can energize them towards motivation. As orange is the colour of moving forward.

It also helps restore and regeneration the cells releasing stagnated energy so the person can allow creativity to shine through. Communication is helped with orange especially in the counselling setting .Talking releases the methadone taker from the fears that have bound them in the past. Organize their confused thoughts, thus freeing them to retake their power raising their spirit. Spirit is missing in methadone use as drugs smother the personality, hiding it beneath a Choke of synthetic substances; the colour orange enhances movement while gently letting the Individual to communicate clearly their intended intentions at change.

This brilliant vibrant colour helps the methadone user stay focused on their intended goals, while encouraging the breaking of addictive habits like smoking, drinking caffeine, chocolate and alcohol. By encouraging new lifestyle patterns the methadone user is able to advance in the direction needed to break the cycle of addiction.

Oranges' are a rich source of vitamin C, which can help diminish the deep set lines that resemble crevices on methadone users faces. This wonder vitamin C is important in helping the methadone takers immune system to manufacture antibody production, encouraging a natural

Progression of resistance to infection to take place. Vitamin C is a must for colds, fl u, cough's, muscles.

By wearing orange you can influence the confidence to change, for the methadone a bowl of hot tomato soup, or orange lentils, carrot soup can lighten the budget while affording you the privilege of receiving the protein needed to help the body make the much needed amino acids that fuels neurotransmitters.

An orange scarf wrapped about your neck shall help ward off the dreaded flu, Drink freshly squeezed orange juice each morning as it contains both the vitamins and minerals needed to help regeneration of cells, as oranges contain both calcium, potassium, manganese, pectin, fibre and zinc. The latter is extremely important in the immune system while fibre can help with constipation that over all burden that afflicts those on methadone. By supplementing their diet with some oranges they not only get the much needed support of cleansing the body of a build up of toxic waste but compliment the immune system with the manufacture of antibodies needed to fight hepatitis and HIV.By maximising a balanced diet they contribute to good health. Dried apricots while orange in colour are not as healthy as fresh fruit mainly because it contains certain chemicals to preserve it. Apricots, raisings, sultanas, can be sprayed with sulphur dioxide rendering them unsuitable for consumption

These dried foods must be washed toughly before eating.

Fresh they are a great vitamin booster as they contain ABC iron, potassium, manganese magnesium, helping to create healthy bones, fight conditions connected to the upper respiratory tract, plus helping the largest organ in the body the skin.

Carrots also a member of the orange family can be taken in liquid form, mixed with apples these health boosters are a must for good health. The juice of the carrots is extracted from the pulp which can then be utilized and used in a salad or recycled as fertilizer.

Orange Peppers are a must when stuffed with whole grain brown rice and spinach they make a great healthy meal for methadone users.

Purple is a colour of spiritually evoking a sense of fulfilment. Deep, mysterious, and sultry the colour purple is associated with humanity. It is my saviour in times of conflict bringing contentment in one's own skin. Independent it connects mind, body and spirit, Choice, responsibility, accepting consequences for ones actions, maturity, philosophy, holiness, pure, Herbs associated with this royal colour are lavender, a natural antiseptic that intercepts the dreaded hospital bug but its properties are not yet accepted by some in the scientific c world Purple helps the methadone user to advance by dispelling the negativity that hunts them daily, it manifests self belief, grounds, heals, advantages in interests ,encouraging, destroys the fears and distrust in others . Yoga meditation, setting standards by example in their communities. The herb lavender can be grows in tubs or drape a border along a path as a protective measure in any methadone house hold. These glorious scented flowers can dispel all negativity as it wharfs below the nose of methadone takers, smell is associated with drug taking and most of -those who come off heroin shall comment on the difficult they experience when confronter and accosted daily by drug pushers, the smell of the white dust that has made its way halfway across the world is enough for the abstainer to lose their best kept intention. This natural healer can be dabbed on a tissue and smelled each time temptation raises its ugly head for the courageous person partaking of the opium's second cousin methadone. Individually is the street the methadone taker is trying to reach, it is this same street that the dealer must control to make his profit in human suffering, for every methadone taker that makes it ,the dealer loses power and his or her false sense of self- esteem and importance. Insomnia is a common occurrence when taking methadone, this lack of sleep is treated in the medical professional way of drugs, while these are necessary in cases of sleep deprivation these strong medication is not suitable for long term use as they have serious side effects for the user. It is now common knowledge that drinking milky substances at bedtime increases the serotonin levels needed to manufacture the neurotransmitter that promotes sleep.

This discovery prompts the question could those taking methadone have low serotonin levels which was dealt with at the beginning of this book.

Music can also prepare methadone takers for sleep music that calms can be some classical tunes that bought in healing and crystal shops.

Wear purple nightwear of spray the room with lavender oil about 2 hours before retiring for the night.

Yellow or gold is the colour associated with prosperity, luck, sun, relaxation, wisdom, material wealth. Archangel Gabriel, Self worth, protection, balance, exercise, travel, confidence, creativity, or predictable. Yellow is associated with helping all conditions to do with the bowel. Inflammation, digestive system. As stated thought out this book one of the negative uses of indulging in drug use is hepatitis and HIV/ AIDS this disease was spread by sharing needles. Once acquired this disease if left undiagnosed can destroy the liver. Yellow is said to help the immune system to fight infection probably due to the sun's rays which have certain healing vitamins.

Certain fruit and vegetables contain these vitamins and trace minerals essential for cell growth. Most vegetables have enzymes essential for the digestive system, while others destroy chemicals in the body. Dopamine is a natural chemical in the brain, an excess can be responsible for certain mental health disorders like schizophrenia, while a decrease of serotonin leads to depression. We also saw in an earlier capture how sunlight is a must for both humans and plants to foster the much needed zinc, potassium. A depletion of zinc in the soil can have devastating effects on human's health. Enzymes are proteins that when broken down to produce the amino acids the brain and body needs to maintain harmony. Raw food is higher in enzymes than preferable over cooked. Metabolism is regulated by an intake of vegetables and fruits as is sprouts, beans and seeds. Most sprouts contain RNA nucleic acid found in all living cells and DNA nucleic acids for genetic instructions. Sprouts are not only cost effective but are delicious in summer salads and soups and juices.

These health builders can help those taking methadone to strengthen the liver and bile to Excrete the daily build up of toxins.

Alfalfa sprouts have a rich nutritional value of folic acid, calcium, zinc, fibre, copper, not only are these wonderful but under-rated foods high in energy and help with destroying free radicals.

About the Author

May Cassidy has worked in the field of addiction for over ten years? She holds a BA. Pysc. H.dip. M.A. I AAAP.

She runs a successful counseling and holistic centre while continuing to work in a methadone programme. She is an accomplished Author having published a number of books. May also makes her own organic oils and creams.